A Replacement Son

The Story of Being a Prisoner to Expectations and Circumstance

BY

Justin Tyler White

First Edition-Retail Sales

A Replacement Son

Justin Tyler White

First Edition: April 2022

Published by: Bluegrass New Classics

Info@TheLossPros.com

Hebron Ky 41048

Typesetting: Justin White

Book Design: by Justin White

Cover Design: Olayemi Bolaji

A CIP record for this book is available from the Library of Congress Cataloging-in-Publication Data

ISBN-13: 978 0-578-36618-0

Printed in USA

Dedicated To:

Allison, Hailey, Keller, and Jacob

Foreword

Robberies, Stabbings, High-Speed Car Chases, Kidnappings……My life reads like a true-crime novel. And it's all true. It all happened, every last detail, but reading this book isn't going to give you the whole story. On average, it may only be 75% accurate. This inaccuracy isn't because I'm making anything up or filling in the blanks for color or drama. The inaccuracies exist because I am the one writing it; you, as the reader, are only getting the story from one perspective, mine.

If you ask a cop or prosecutor what the truth is about a particular event, a good one will refuse to answer. Instead, they will say there are three sides to the story, his side, her side, and the truth. While the particular roles and instances may change when applying this reasoning to events in our lives, the lesson persists. Facts and real "Truth"(big T) exist separately from how anyone remembers or experiences an event. This doesn't make anyone's personal truth (little t) less accurate it's just that it only exists for them and is not shared by others.

This is the same phenomenon that allows trauma victims to recall the details and circumstances of a given event in a much different way than the perpetrators. These recollections can vary so much that in some cases, both parties to an event view themselves as a victim of the other; their versions are so different they can't even agree on who the victim was. Are they wrong? Who knows? I'm sure it depends on the facts first, but if it exists, the blame will ultimately fall on how each victim feels about the event. Maybe they are both victims of two slightly different traumas perpetrated by the other. Perhaps in normal circumstances, these events wouldn't even be considered traumas but not for the history and prior experiences of the parties involved.

Consider the example of a child who is teased for wearing red sweatpants to school every day. It is possible that the pants are the only pair that the child has, and they have no choice but to wear them every day. Or maybe the child is autistic and chooses to wear that particular style and color of pants because they don't have a tag and are comfortable. They actually have several pairs of the same style and color. They wear a different pair every day that just appears to be the same pair. In both scenarios, the kids teasing are in the wrong. That is a fact (T) that exists regardless of how people feel about it. However, the degree to which the exact words traumatize the recipients can vary greatly(t).

I suspect that the autistic child doesn't even acknowledge the teasing because, from their perspective, they choose to wear comfortable pants, and it's a fresh pair each day. Since, from their perspective, there is no merit to the teasing, the net effect of the teasing is negligible.

The child who only has one pair is likely to feel terrible about the teasing. They are being victimized twice, once by the adult who isn't providing a proper wardrobe, and again by the teasing kids. This child may even be a victim a third time by a teacher who hasn't bothered stepping in despite noticing the issue.

The facts are that kids tease other children because they appear to be wearing the same clothes every day. That's the only Truth(T) in this scenario. They can tease every day, and if they do it to one kid, they aren't traumatizing or otherwise harming that child (t). However, if they do it to the second kid, they traumatize that child directly. They are contributing to the re-victimization and compounding the neglect of that child. The victims' truths (t) vary greatly despite having experienced the same set of facts (T). This divide is because of the experiences and circumstances that make up each victim, not a difference in facts.

Why did I give the previous example? I did it to illustrate that we are all a combination of our experiences and circumstances. Some of those are big T truths that are objective and fact-based, and others are little t's that are more about our reactions to things than the actual thing. The goal is to decipher better which ones matter and which ones we have control over. You can't control facts(T), but you can control how you feel about facts(t). Sometimes your perception of the event changes as you experience new things, which can shift to the positive or negative, but regardless of where they shift, they will pivot around the big T truths.

At this point, you have been given glimpses into the chaos that was my life. There are many more stories of mayhem and a few of redemption along the way. I will follow a chronological order with specific years provided when possible(T). Some identities are genuine, and others have been changed to protect those involved. This isn't a self-help book, nor is it meant to be inspirational or—God forbid—instructional. I would be genuinely concerned for anyone who looked at my choices as inspirational. Instead, it is meant to demonstrate how I managed to survive the trauma and come out on the other side as a mostly functional, real live human being. I am a sum of all of my experiences (T) and my perceptions and reactions (t). Over time the impact of both has shifted and changed, but I am living proof that you can harness the negatives and turn them into positives. My life demonstrates precisely that, and I am sharing my story is to show that it is possible to make that change; what you do with this example is up to you.

During the book, I have written each chapter with a voice and perspective that is authentic for that period in time. If I am successful, you may see my views and attitudes change as we progress, which is the point. From time to time, I will also close the chapters off with what I was able to take away from that event or period in time. Whatever I share won't be the only thing I learned, and it's entirely possible I picked up some bad lessons along the way.

So many people from my generation have been shielded from some of the more egregious traumas that were more common in the past. They find themselves unsure if they can overcome the next "worst thing that has ever happened in my life." Just how bad is that new "worst thing"? The measure of degree is subjective and different for each person experiencing it. That isn't to say that younger people don't experience real and significant traumas. It is simply saying that all too often, the severity of the event is not adequately tempered with the benefit of time or experience that is needed to make such a judgment. Younger people instead let the existence of the trauma (T) be the defining element of their life when they have no control over that part. The reality is that the characteristic that defines their life is how they feel about that trauma(t), and they have complete control over that part. You can't change what happens to you, but you sure in the hell can change how you let that event affect your life.

Chapter 1

Raccoons Fist Fights and Paperwork

I stood at the top of the back stairs, looking left then right. It was hushed; the only sound I could hear over my pounding heart was the muted lessons behind the closed classroom doors. The carpeted halls made this school different from any of my previous ones—it was devoid of the neat and orderly 12x12 tiles that would echo every sound. I quietly counted down in my head, 11:57…11:58…waiting for just the right moment, the anticipation killing me. Just then, the sickly electronic tone crackled across the second-rate PA system. I could hear the doors bursting open; now was the time if I was going to do it. I looked around one last time to make sure I wasn't seen. Slowly, I grabbed the zipper and pulled. I had done it with the deliberate and notchy sliding of the zipper. I had opened my backpack and released chaos.

I am not sure how I expected the following minutes to unfold, but I had already accomplished my mission in my mind. I had convinced myself I would get away, escaping any blame. I quickly walked in the opposite direction as innocently as possible while ten pounds of angry Procyon Lotor (Raccoon) ravaged the lower classman hallway. I didn't have any specific expectations for what would happen after its release, but what ensued exceeded anything I could have imagined. This raccoon was angry, and rightfully so; he had been contained in a backpack for several hours after being trapped in a wire cage the night before. This robust specimen seemed to possess a particularly strong will to survive—he was the Marcus Luttrell of raccoons. Alone in enemy territory without weapons or comrades, he decided his only way out was to fight, and fight he did. The way this raccoon could charge a crowd of high school boys was magical. First, he would do the raccoon run straight towards the group, then he stood up on his hind legs and spread his little paws while making raccoon noises. He would then alternate between making another charge or trying to seek shelter on the top of the lockers. While he was an excellent climber, he was no match for the smooth steel panels positioned at 45-degree angles on top of the lockers. These plates were just as effective at keeping raccoons off as they were stray backpacks. He was eventually cornered after sliding off a section of lockers. This is where he made his last stand; cornered in front of Mrs. Callen's door, he was tackled by at least two boys. The raccoon had latched onto the hand of a sophomore named Mike and was sinking his tiny raccoon teeth down to the bone. Mike came up screaming and holding the raccoon. Stumbling to his feet, he ran for the door. I can still see the little guy gnawing on Mike's hand, biting a little deeper each time he clenched. Mike eventually got to the door and flung the ring-tailed bandit free. After making his best Rocky (the flying squirrel, not the boxer) impression, the raccoon scampered into the woods, never to be seen again.

Two fun facts that were relevant to that day's events

1. A raccoon's closest living relative is a bear. This makes a raccoon a little grizzly wearing a bandit mask. They can be just as fierce as a grizzly when corned, as poor Mike found out. This grizzly attitude would also explain the Lone Survivor-like fight the little guy put up during his escape.
2. To test a wild animal for rabies after it has bitten some-

one, you need the animal. There is no test you can do on the victim of the bite. You either need the animal who did the biting, or you must assume the animal had rabies and proceed with a course of painful shots to the stomach. Sorry, Mike.

Within five minutes, it was all over—at least the initial wave of commotion. The bell rang, and everyone not injured or investigating the aftermath filed into their classes, including me. I made it to my next class—tenth grade English. Relieved, I acted as if nothing had happened and settled in. The dialogue in my head must have gone something like, "no one saw you; that raccoon could have come from anywhere; maybe they should be more worried about the maintenance if they don't want raccoons running around." Within thirty minutes, I was sitting in the principal's office. Apparently showing off a live raccoon that you had been holding captive in your backpack to a dozen people before school isn't a model for discretion, especially when a few hours later you intend to release the very same raccoon with the sole intent of creating havoc. Never fear; I was no stranger to trouble and had seen my fair share of principals' offices over the years. By the time I found myself in Mr. Keen's office, I was a veteran. I had picked up my education in the administrative arts from the school of hard knocks. This would be the third principal's office I had found myself sitting inside of in 1997. Leading up to that faithful day, I had attended no less than three different institutions my sophomore year.

The first school was Conner High School, a reasonably sized public school in my district. My attendance was cut short that year by a fistfight and subsequent altercation with the gym teacher. While the conflict's particulars are lost to history, it seemed related to the teacher aiding my adversary's escape.

The second school of the year was Anderson High School. My attendance at that posh public campus was predicated on borrowing an out-of-state address from a family friend. This auspicious start quickly evolved into the kind of ending you would expect. I had been expelled for "allegedly" possessing fake parking passes by the beginning of spring break. I say allegedly because they were, in fact, genuine parking passes; they just weren't issued to me or the dozen or so people I sold them to. My real downfall could be pinned on the fact that I had driven a classic Corvette I had borrowed from my grandfather to school one day. The car was a beautiful 1972 model with metallic gold paint, T-tops, a supped-up engine, and an obnoxiously loud exhaust. I knew I couldn't park it in the student lot, so I chose the next best option: I parked it in the teacher's lot. An obnoxious Corvette with out-of-state plates and a parking pass of dubious origins—you can imagine how well that went. By the end of that day, I found myself school-less for the second time in as many semesters.

Quickly running out of options, I suggested to my grandpa that maybe we could do a private school. I reasoned that while they could always tell you no at a public school, that you didn't pay for, it was a lot harder to do so when you were paying for the pleasure of attending. By the following Monday, I was enrolled at a somewhat prestigious private school called Covington Catholic. Yep, that Covington Catholic, home of at least one Olympian and a more recently famous viral video star. The school had been turning out great graduates for nearly 100 years and was notorious for having high expectations of behavior from its students. What could go wrong?

Back in the principal's office, while I was explaining myself to Mr. Keen, I passed up a perfect get-out-of-jail-free card. As most high schools do, we had a crazy biology teacher who always rescues or saves animals—ours was Mr. Rolf. I should have said I had found the raccoon injured and was going to bring it to Mr. Rolf so he could nurse it back to health, but before I got it to him, it had managed to escape. While plausible, this story was still full of holes—like why was the raccoon was so pissed off, you had biology earlier in the day, so why didn't you give it to him then, and so forth.

In the end, I admitted my involvement in the great raccoon conspiracy of '97. I was confident my punishment would be trivial as I ultimately did the right thing and confessed to my participation. I was excused out of the office and told to sit down, presumably while I waited for the paperwork. Twenty minutes turned into an hour and then two. My stomach began to sink as I knew what that meant. As this was my third school of the year, the reality of what was happening quickly set in.

For those of you who aren't school terrorists, there are different levels of getting in trouble at school. Everyone is familiar with the first level, including basics such as detention or Saturday school. Those were handled via a quick talk with the principal and the issuing of a neat little slip or maybe a two-part carbon copy form. Once you had the form, you'd be sent back to class to think about **how** and, in some cases, **if** you were going to deliver the news to your parents.

The second level of trouble was suspension. It typically involved a form with a description of the reported act and possibly a recitation of your previous relevant actions. There was almost always a phone call to a parent, and unless it happened very early in the day before classes started, you still got sent back to class. The result was that you could be excluded somewhere between one to ten whole days. It is my theory that the limited-reasoning abilities possessed by most principals generally kept them from being able to calculate appropriate punishments on a partial-day basis. This lack of cognitive ability left full instructional days as the only options to extract their pound of flesh. The filling out of this form and the calling of the parents takes a little bit of time and usually has you sitting back in the waiting area for ten to twenty minutes before you can resume your day.

This brings us to the third level of punishment. It involved a form with a lengthy section for a description of the events, names of witnesses, inventory of property damaged and was almost always served up in triplicate with various pink, yellow, and white copies to be subsequently stored as part of your permanent record in some vault controlled by the school board. As I sat in the waiting room for an hour, I knew what was coming. I could imagine Mr. Keen filling out the form. Description of Events: releasing of a yet-to-be-confirmed rabid raccoon in the freshman hallway.....Witness: the whole damn school plus a few more that saw the raccoon in a backpack earlier.......Description of Damage: raccoon feces everywhere, student victims' blood dripped on the carpet....Injuries: Mike S. was badly bitten on the hand by a raccoon with superman strength, will need a course of rabies shots...Recommended Action: send him down the road; no amount of money makes it worth keeping him around.

This was the third school of my sophomore year. By my actions, I'd found myself either precisely where I wanted to be or maybe precisely where I deserved to be—waiting on that long-form with all the copies. I was getting expelled for the third time that year. At the end of the day, my grandpa, Russell, showed up at school, and we were ushered back into the principal's office. Russell was at that time about sixty-four to sixty-five years old. He had a tall, barrel-chested frame but the demeanor and presence of a teddy bear. That's not to say he couldn't be a grizzly when he had to, but he was a push-over nine times out of ten.

The principal handed over our copy of the form and something I had never seen before. It was a letter on official-looking letterhead. It was a few paragraphs long, stating that I was being expelled. The letter, however, wasn't that raw in its delivery. As this was a prestigious private school, they were very clever about how they conveyed the message. "Unfortunately, Mr. White will not be invited back next year to continue his education." One of the more memorable lessons from that day was that you could take a simple idea like being expelled and spin that into a considerably more elegant and less offensive "not invited back." The whole process of being kicked out, which already stung, was made worse because I had even paid to be admitted in the first place. By kicking me out of school, they were really saying even though you pay us to put up with him, we still don't want him back here.

With the elegant softening of the message and by leaving certain finer points unsaid, they had handed me rejection with class. In my mind, back then, I probably took some solace in the fact they were idiots and couldn't take a joke. I'm sure I even quipped back, "Invited back? What makes you think I wanted to be invited in the first place?"

That day was the last day of my high school career; I was sixteen years old and adrift. High school didn't end with graduation for me. There was no prom or homecoming dance. It ended with a rather mediocre display of chaos courtesy of a nocturnal friend. I'm sure I received some sort of punishment at the time from Russell, but for the life of me, I can't remember what it was. I'm sure Mike's rabies shots lasted longer than any punishment that came my way.

My mom heard about everything a few days later but didn't outwardly react. She wasn't mad or much of anything at that point, as our relationship had deteriorated and morphed into something very different. What was left between us was part guilt and part resignation towards the relationship lost. She knew we would never be able to have a normal parental relationship, but she still wanted to look out and care for me the best she could. Fueled by guilt or the need to prove she could indeed be a good mother; she went to work.

My mother always had a way of working the system and finding loopholes. Her whole life was spent on the edge of legality with multiple drivers' licenses in different names and various accounts, identities, and personas. There was always some exception or get-out-of-jail-free card she could pull if push came to shove. She somehow signed me up for adult GED classes using her infinitely flexible sense of justice and persuasion skills. Mind you, I was only sixteen at the time, and my lack of attendance at any school was due to me being expelled, not from dropping out. I went to the first class and finished the session teaching others there. I immediately signed up for the GED, the test was supposed to be taken over several hours across two days. I was done with the whole thing in less than an hour, and just like that, I had my GED. At the time, I viewed that little piece of paper as a giant waste of time—and it was. It didn't have grades or scores; it simply said PASSED. I have shown it on precisely two occasions my entire life—up until this point. Once, when I registered for college classes, and once when I was filling out information for a background check at a big, fancy corporate job. Had I not had that stupid piece of paper, I likely would have never bothered with college classes and may not have been able to get that fancy job that paid more than a quarter of a million dollars a year. So, by some strange twist of fate and karma, I am eternally grateful for her forcing me to take that stupid test following the great Raccoon Controversy of '97.

Chapter 2

First Memories: Guns, Drugs, Stabbings, and a Little Rock & Roll

We all have a first memory, and often that first memory has a way of shifting or being elusive to its timing. We can often recall the minor details so vividly yet can't remember the context or when it happened no matter how hard we try. My wife—who you will get to know later—says her first memory was waking up in the hospital, not from when she was born, but later when she had a rare form of tuberculosis and spent months at the hospital. She vividly recalls how friendly the nurses were to her and how much she hated being in bed. Technically speaking, this can't be her first memory as she also recalls a family member noticing the lump on her neck that inevitably led to her being in the hospital, but through the magic of first memories, if you ask her what her first memory is, her automatic answer is waking up in the hospital. I suspect everyone's first memories follow a similar paradox. From a technical perspective, they may not be first memories, but for whatever reason, they become identified as such because of their impact on young minds.

Professionals have explained this phenomenon to me, research has shown that people remember an event's emotion, and our minds fill in all the details for context. That is to say, without some emotional charge or trigger at the core; our minds might not even bother with cataloging and documenting the relevant details. This would also imply that the more emotional or impactful, the more information and surrounding relevant information gathered by our minds. I assume the relationship between emotion and detail contributes to my nearly photographic recollection of my early childhood.

The first four years of my life happened at an apartment complex known today as Cambridge Square. It was a typical section 8 apartment with a two-bedroom layout that has been repeated in thousands of similar complexes. You walked into the dining room/living room combo when you stepped through the door. The kitchen was to the left, a small galley affair with a pantry at the end. Down the hallway, there were two closets, one for towels and linens and another narrow one for storing the drugs and money. My room was on the right, and my mom's room was at the end of the hall. The address was 107 Promontory, Apartment F; it was the last building in the back right of the complex. You entered from a sidewalk that placed you on the middle level of the building, the same floor as our apartment. Walking into the building was always jarring, with loud echoes, sounds of doors slamming, and stray shouting assaulting your senses. Aside from the sounds, you were instantly hit with the smell of weed, paint, and roaches in that order.

The origin of the weed and paint smells were self-explanatory. Weed resulted from our small, home-based enterprise and the paint was from the constant turnover of tenants moving in and out. I also suspect the maintenance team figured it was cheaper to paint the walls with its 256th coat of sickly off-white paint than actually to spray for bugs. If you didn't grow up poor, you might not know what roaches smell like, but they have a distinct aroma. It's a cross between a sticky, sweet smell and cheap paneling like you would find in an old mobile home or poorly remodeled basement. On top of their scent, roaches have two other defining characteristics."

1. They defecate on everything, leaving behind tiny, telltale brown spots that get impossibly stuck to whatever surface it lands on.

2. Wherever there are roaches, there are people spraying pesticides to get rid of them.

The only ones living in this apartment at the time were my mom and me. She was about nineteen or twenty, beautiful with long, black, curly hair, tan skin, and glasses. She was a lot like a cross between Esmeralda and Janice Joplin. She was a rock and roll girl bordering on groupie. At that point in her life, she was solidly in the post-hippie music phase but not embracing disco or '80s pop just yet. Like her personality, her wardrobe had two separate and intense flavors—either she was casually dressed in a pair of jeans and a t-shirt or exotically in a long, flowing dresses with lots of dangling jewelry and belts. That was if she was wearing any clothes at all, nudity or partial nudity abbreviated with only a robe or housecoat could be considered a 3rd flavor that was nearly as common as the others.

I can't remember my dad or any other consistent guy living with us. I remember several guys being around, but it was never a consistent guy, just consistent company. If I had to describe my relationship with my mom, I would use partners-in-crime or adventure-buddies. That may seem a little odd, but I remember almost everything we did together back then as some sort of journey or adventure. We may not have known exactly where we were going or where we would end up, but it certainly had every indication of being an adventure or very possibly a crime.

We didn't have tons of furniture, but my room had a bed and a toy box made of plywood painted red with my name on the front in white letters. I distinctly remember a small table made out of an old cable spool. It sat about eighteen inches high and was just big enough for a child-sized chair to sit next to it. I'm not sure of the guy's name who brought it, but it was a gift from one of the more regular guy-friends that would come around. The living room was pretty empty with a single couch, a small, oval-shaped coffee table, and an old, tube-type B&W TV in the corner. Interestingly enough, I recall that the TV only had one knob out of the original three, probably lost through time or a violent outburst. If you wanted higher UHF channels or to change the volume, you had to pull the knob off and reinstall it on the other post to operate.

In terms of toys, I remember having a few favorites. I had a blue stuffed bear that made a melodic chime as you shook him—much like a dog toy. I had a few toy monster trucks that were battery-powered, and once turned on, they would go and go until they got tangled in something or found their way into a crevice or crack, lost forever. I vividly remember the trucks, particularly the adventures my mom and I had to get them. I had questioned my memory of these adventures for many years as they didn't make much sense. I could recall going to the small grocery store with my mom and stopping by the counter where they sold cosmetics and picking a blue one out. This, of course, doesn't make any sense; why wouldn't I grab one from the toy aisle? Further to that same point, why would a small mom-and-pop grocery store even have a cosmetics counter, a service counter for money orders and cigarettes sure, but not cosmetics?

I was certain about my memory, but it didn't make sense. I could recall the kind of carts that sat high, the layout and locations of certain items, even when we got ice cream cones as a special treat. I could never reconcile how I remembered the adventure with what I knew about grocery stores. A few years ago, bothered by the inconsistency in my memory about that adventure, I searched the Internet and found the answer. The particular toy trucks were called "Stompers." They were not sold on cardboard and clear plastic blister packs like we see for toys now. They were sold in a revolving counter top display made of glass, just like cosmetics, sunglasses, and watches. They included no packaging. You simply picked out the one you wanted, and the cashier handed it to you across the counter with a fresh battery. That truck and a few others purchased in the same way were precious to me. I don't know if it was because I didn't have many toys or if it was the fact that I had gotten them while on an adventure with my mom. Regardless those little trucks were the start of my love for all things motorized.

I had one last possession that technically couldn't be described as a toy but nonetheless led to hours of enjoyment. I previously described the roach infestation present in the building—well, each tenant had their method for dealing with it. Some would wad up aluminum foil in every little gap and crevice. Some would constantly spray pesticides from cans. My mom was partial to roach motels. They are small, open-ended cardboard boxes with sticky glue on the interior if you're not familiar. "Roaches check-in, but they never check out." While everybody's methods had merits, I chose the most direct avenue for a three-year-old.... I had my roach brick. It was precisely that—a brick, or more correctly, about three-quarters of a brick that had previously seen duty as a doorstop. I had re-purposed this standard brick into a smashing machine. Aside from my Stomper truck, it was my favorite toy. I would spend hours chasing, smashing, and ambushing my pesky little friends. While I had smashed my fingers a few times, I kept myself occupied controlling the local roach population for hours.

One evening, I was sitting on the floor, legs crossed, watching TV. I was hot and itchy. I had on a pair of canary-yellow pajamas with white trim and feet. The pajamas were the weird onesie style with a zipper that went up from the foot to the collar. The feet had some sort of plastic or vinyl material that had hardened and cracked with age and would press painfully into my sweaty feet. The polyester fabric had become worn and pilled, the arms were too short, and the zipper wouldn't go up to the top. I remember, above all else, an intense sense of discomfort. I was constrained, trapped, sweaty and itchy—but was I really uncomfortable? I had worn that same pair of pajamas many times, maybe too many...is that why they were too small? All I know for sure is they were my favorite. But why would they be my favorite if they were so uncomfortable?

Suddenly I heard shouting; the front door swung open, slamming into the wall behind it. A man stood there with dark blue jeans that were threadbare and a red and black flannel shirt buttoned nearly to the top with the tail lose. I could see a little of the white undershirt beneath the flannel. The undershirt was off-white or yellowed with age. He had a black ski mask, tight and ribbed, starting at the crown of the head and going down the neck, taught and slightly askew. The mouth and eye holes lined up well enough but weren't perfect. Black leather gloves covered each hand. The gloves had a short cuff that showed a little of the base of the wrist when the arm was extended. A well-worn black metallic revolver was in his right hand. I believe it had a wooden handle. The gun was small in size; I would guess a snub nose .38, the quintessential small revolver used by thugs in the late '70s and '80s. He carried a bag of some sort in his left hand; despite every other detail being vivid and clear, the bag's description or even proportions escaped me. He wore black leather engineer or motorcycle boots, the type with no laces but a buckle and a silver ring on the side where the straps intersect. The black leather gloves and black leather boots somehow hinted to me that they were part of a set or ensemble or, at the very least, pieces of a larger aesthetic.

Holding the gun out straight, he shouted out, "Nobody Move." At least one person was sitting on the couch, in-distinct, un-named, and unremarkable, while my mother stood about eight feet away in the kitchen. In three or four quick steps, the man covered the twelve feet to the wall where the phone was. In one swift motion, he ripped the cord out of the wall jack preventing any calls for help. My mom had her hands up with somewhat bent elbows. She wore a maroon robe made of velour, the breast, and a belt with white piping. The man said, "I want all of it; where is it?" My mom was visibly upset and scared, but she didn't hesitate; she quickly took him to the narrow closet where we stored it. At that point, everything was happening out of my sight down the hall. I could hear my mom screaming, but it didn't sound entirely in fear, but more like anger. I inched towards the coffee table and hid underneath. I looked up and saw green crayon marks and a cheap, blue, stick-on air freshener underneath. The crayon marks were mine, and the air freshener had always been there as far as I knew. A few seconds later, the man left as fast as he had come in, taking only a few more steps to cover the entire length of the apartment. He wasn't running, just taking long, deliberate strides. My mom ran to the door and slammed it closed. I heard the frantic speed and deliberate swish the security chain made before she slid it into the slot. The person on the couch looked shocked and didn't say a word. My mom quickly picked me up as she sobbed. I don't remember crying; I'm sure I did, but maybe not. I remember everything else vividly, all the way down to the smell of the shitty air freshener. After all, how big of a stretch is it to think maybe I hadn't cried? Perhaps I had been used to that sort of thing, essentially conditioned by my environment to just roll with whatever came my way. I had probably been conditioned to take my cues from those around me as to how to behave, silent and still just like the coward of a man that was sitting on the couch.

Looking back on the events that night, I can't help but notice what I did remember and what I didn't; memories are strange like that. They are odd regarding what details they include, such as the scent of an air freshener, and what they leave out, like the bag's color and style. This variability always leaves you wondering what you really saw versus what you remember. You can never be sure of what really happened based on a single memory. Memory also has another quirk; it loves patterns and repetition. When you have something important to remember, many people repeat that thing repeatedly, developing patterns and repetition. Likewise, if you hear a phone number repeatedly, you're likely able to remember that number. Behaviors and patterns work the same way. Like Pavlov's dog, humans can be trained to expect specific outcomes based on cues or observations. This can go a step further in which people engage in certain behaviors, expecting these behaviors will have a particular outcome. I wonder how much of my life can be distilled down to memories and patterns of repetition.

Earlier I had mentioned that sometimes first memories really weren't first but instead may have just been BIG. Unfortunately, that isn't my case. I know that to be fact because I have also experienced the second quirk of memory—repetition. I wish I could say my childhood was punctuated by that single traumatic night, but it wasn't. I experienced nights like that repeatedly. I even took ownership of the enterprise in my memories. My mom didn't get robbed—**WE** got robbed. It was only natural that I felt some connection to the business as it was the basis for many of my memories. I even had my own special job. At the time, it was popular for small-scale growing operations to place their plants inside the fields of legitimate farmers. This way, you get all the benefits of tilled soil, watering, and fertilizers without the risk. It's hard to notice a few plants in the center of a forty-acre cornfield; they were invisible if you didn't know where to look. This was a time when helicopter patrols to spot these operations weren't as common, as they are today. I learned the most significant risk to our crops was not the police or the farmers but rather the rabbits and deer. That's where I came in. My job was to pee around the plants so the rabbits and deer wouldn't eat them. Looking back, I realize what my real job was—and it wasn't an animal deterrent—but I will never forget it as precisely that.

If my job wasn't pest control, then what was it, you may ask? I was the decoy, the sympathetic get-out-of-jail-free card. If we were ever discovered when we harvested, it was easy to pretend like we were just a family out hiking that had gotten lost. They could always say I had got lost in the cornfield, and they were worried sick looking for me. I even served as the ultimate backup of all backups, the get-out-of-jail-free card. Before the national war on drugs, a county sheriff or disgruntled farmer could be swayed by a young blond-haired, blue-eyed boy who would wind up an orphan if his mom were to be arrested. I watched that trick work at least once when caught harvesting and another time when my mom had been caught driving drunk with me in the car. Now that you have gotten your first lesson in Weed 101 taught by a four-year-old, let's get back to memories and how they get so much clearer with repetition.

Growing up as I did, loud fights and screaming weren't uncommon. Nearly any event could turn into a screaming, knock-down, drag-out fight complete with pushing, hitting, and even throwing. In particular, I remember one battle that had my mom throwing a frying pan full of refried beans at my dad. I'm not sure what made this fight memorable, maybe it was the eventual outcome, or perhaps it was related to the wasting of food. Despite the nature of our income, we never seemed to have an abundance of food. I remember many canned goods such as **SOUP** and dry goods like **PASTA**. This was back in the good old days when it was still okay to shame poor people and make them use monopoly money food stamps to buy generic items in white boxes with government stencil letters spelling out the contents like **PASTA** and **RICE.** We always seemed to have a package of government **CHEESE** in the fridge, and my mom's favorite treat to make for me was ghetto nachos. Her version was made with a round tortilla chip dolloped with refried beans topped with a sliver of government **CHEESE** and jalapeños on hers.

That night was one of the rare times I can remember my dad being at the apartment. My mom was making my nachos, and they had started arguing. He had gone back to the bedroom and found something amiss. This was where the stash closet was and where we kept all of the drugs; I assume it was some inventory issue that bothered him. It could have been any number of things, but I'm going with the inventory issue for brevity. A screaming fight quickly escalated into a pushing and smacking affair. I had intellectually backed away into the living room; moments later, my mom had grabbed the hot pan off the stove threw it at my dad. She just missed his head, but beans went everywhere. The pan was bent nearly in half after hitting the wall, having been thrown with full force using the handle for leverage. She was enraged and just getting started.

Contrary to cultural norms, it had never been my experience that my dad was the aggressor. In fact, over the years, I would come to know a side of my mom and her anger that would shock all but the most hardened fighters. She had anger and aggression that could instantly be escalated to the use of weapons, whether that be her fingernails, a can of corn, or an embellished belt, all of which I have seen used at various times. That day, her weapon of choice was a steak knife with a wooden handle about eight inches long overall and serrated on one edge. I don't know if she chose the knife for lethality or convenience as it was close at hand, having been used to cut thin slices of government cheese off the block moments before. She spun around and plunged that knife into dad's back in an instant. She came from above, landing somewhere between his clavicle and shoulder blade. I assume she hit bone as her hand slid down the handle, and she'd also cut herself.

I vividly remember the blood. The sight and smell of it. The way it looked as it dripped on the floor into messy dots, thick and dark in the center with tiny splashes radiating out. I remember her, half bent over, holding her hand as the blood ran down. I remember the sound of tears and screams coming from her all simultaneously. She had pulled the knife out, but he had managed to knock it from her bloody hand to the floor. My dad instantly snatched me up and took me to the car. He jumped in, still bleeding, and we peeled out. In any other circumstance, I would have loved the sound of tires screeching and the smell of rubber burning, but this wasn't an ordinary trip. In this circumstance, I was in shock, and squalling tires and burning rubber weren't going to make it better.

There were no police or child services, not even neighbors; it was just him and me, and he didn't know what to do. Finding himself in the unfamiliar territory of having just performed his only known fatherly duty, he was at a loss for what to do next. My dad eventually took me to my grandparents' house (my mom's mom and stepdad). My grandma, a nurse, proceeded to stitch him up while he sat on the toilet in the bathroom. I remember watching in fascination as she made one neat little stitch after another on his back as he winced in pain. By the end of the operation, I became bored with my sewing lesson and began playing with his jacket, poking my little finger through the hole. He had the kind of heavy black leather jacket a motorcycle guy might wear if he wanted it to match his boots and gloves. That was the last night I lived with my mom for many years. The following day, I went with my grandparents to see my mom and pick up my stuff, of which there was very little. The cut on her hand was big and deep; the knife had cut the webbing between her thumb and hand, extending into the palm. My grandma patched her up, and we left. I would see my mom and dad occasionally after that night. Over the years, my dad's visits would gradually taper off into nothing. My mom's visitation would continue with a gradual ebb and flow correlated to her mental state.

As I recall the events of that time in my life, I am keenly aware of what I can and can't remember. I can remember everything about the robbery and the stabbing in full, living color. I can remember the smells and sounds of the apartment. Even the general nature of the life I lived at that time how it was perfectly normal for your mom to have a "Diet Scale" with gram level precision on the counter. How the burning of incense in every shape and size just to hide the odor of weed was commonplace and accepted as normal and okay. As an adult with slightly enhanced sources of information, I believe I know what happened those two fateful nights. I think the real story is as follows:

My mom and father had initiated the weed growing business. At some point, my dad became indisposed either through incarceration (I visited him in jail once around that time with her) or circumstance. My mom became involved with an old boyfriend who had consistently played as a second-class love interest. This runner-up guy assisted my mom in making a final harvest of what was ultimately my dad and mom's crop. After somehow becoming aware of the harvest and its circumstance, my dad had a significant altercation with the runner-up guy offscreen that I learned about much later in life. I do not believe it was the runner-up guy who was on the couch the night of the robbery because if it had been, my memory would likely have been that of the night of the murder instead of the robbery. I believe my dad then proceeded to rob my mom. I don't know if she knew it was him or if the shock was too much. Still, I am convinced it was him for the following reasons: he knew exactly where everything was, he didn't actually use any violence, only the threat, he spoke very little—likely out of fear of being recognized and because who in the hell wears a full ski mask to a low-level weed robbery in the '80s unless you don't want people who know you to recognize you.

It was the aftermath of this event that led to the stabbing. I suspect I was with my dad earlier that day, but I can't be sure. When my mom and dad were arguing, it was centered on the stash closet. It's my theory he feigned anger towards the missing inventory, and it was the fact she knew damn well it had been him that had robbed us that had set her off the way it did. He still had a leather jacket on, and he couldn't have been at the apartment long or planned to stay long. As an adult, it is my impression that about a month or two had passed between the first robbery incident and the second stabbing incident, but it could have been as short as a few days. I confronted my father with my childhood memories and my adult version of the events but did not get a meaningful response. He was quick to express astonishment that I remembered that stuff and offered sincere regret, but we did not discuss the details further.

It's a funny thing how memory works. The robbery and stabbing couldn't have been my first memories. I never participated in a harvest again after the stabbing. Yet, I know the details of the harvest, so logic tells me the memories of the harvest technically preceded the robbery and stabbing. But if anyone asks me what my first memory is, I will always default to the stabbing or robbery. Do we as humans file our memories based on impact versus time? Or do we do something a little different and retroactively select the memories that make the most sense or somehow support the identity we most want to be true? Is it somehow more offensive to my psyche to be the roach brick kid than the one who got to watch some terrible stuff go down a few times? I'm not ashamed of any of them and will gladly share the stories if asked, but somehow, I feel that a tiny fraction of me takes more comfort in the chaos than the mundane.

Chapter 3

Grandparents: A Danger Adjacent Safe Place

Gloria Dean (Granny) and Russel Lee Hodge (Papaw) were married on August 26th, 1976. It was Gloria's third and Russell's second marriage. Russell had no children of his own, while Gloria had three from a previous marriage that had ended in 1963, five years after it started. The children—in order of age —were my mother Katy, my aunt Jenny, and my uncle Billie.

Granny's early life was centered in the Appalachian regions of Kentucky before she eventually moved towards Somerset in central Kentucky. Granny's upbringing was a rigid southern affair that followed a strict Southern Baptist dogma mixed with the clannish and fiercely devout family allegiances common in Appalachia. Either divorced or never married, her mother carried the Chitwood surname until her death sometime in the early 80s. I only briefly interacted with Granny Chitwood (Gloria's mother) as a child. However, brief the memories, they were always fond and usually contained the compulsory southern components of home cooking and sweet tea. Granny's father was a Hunt. As a young child, I only met Claud Hunt once and remembered him as somewhat coarse and gruff. I had always been aware of some measure of the tension between Granny and her father but never had any insight into the root of that tension. The only thing I can further say on the subject is the divide between them seemed like a grudge—the kind of grudge you carry for your entire lifetime, if not generations beyond you. Claud Hunt died in the early 90s. I remember being at the house when Granny got the call that her father had died. She had clenched her fist and squeezed so tight tremors could be seen in her arms. She let out a few muted cries centered somewhere between anger and sadness, and after a few seconds, she began to cry fully, releasing whatever emotions she had bottled up years before. While growing up, I certainly remember seeing Granny cry from time to time, but it was never quite like this.

Papaw was born in Laurel County, Kentucky, in 1932. He was the middle of three brothers—Jasper, Al, and Russell. His family moved to Cincinnati, Ohio, shortly after his birth. Russell's early life centered around the industrial suburbs of Hartwell, Reading, and Lockland, located on the outskirts of Cincinnati. His upbringing was in a very traditional and loving two-parent household. His father (Jasper Sr) died in the early 80s after retiring to a farm in Okeanna, Ohio. Grandma Hodge (Mae) lived into the early 90s on the same farm while her youngest son Al lived next door and the eldest son Jasper a few miles down the road. I have very fond memories of Christmas and Thanksgiving at her farm. Any time there was fishing to be done or woods to be explored, you could bet it was on her farm with Papaw by my side. The farm is still in the family, with one of Jasper's sons living there today.

Papaw stood over six feet tall in his prime; he was muscular and barrel-chested with the appearance of a formidable man. He is one of the strongest people I have ever met. His hands were the thickest I have ever seen. I remember my young hand barely being able to wrap around a single finger of his. Papaw was a veteran drafted to service in the Korean War on November 20th, 1952. During the war, he was stationed primarily in France and Germany. Based on the stories I heard, he mainly served as a Powerman (electrical worker) and spent a fair amount of his time boxing in either official capacities or for sport. He had always been a gentle man, and as a child, I couldn't imagine him ever fighting with anyone. Papaw was always generous to a fault and had a childlike demeanor in its ability to lighten the spirits of anyone he came across. After leaving the Army on October 27th, 1954, as a Corporal, Papaw returned to work at Proctor & Gamble as a chauffeur. By 1959, Papaw had earned his degree in electrical power technology from Ohio Mechanics Institute and became an electrician for P&G. During his thirty-nine-year career at P&G, he did everything from expediting and sourcing machine work to production line installation and heavy electrical maintenance. As a child, it was always fun to hear the work stories about how they built a new bottle washing robot or used a remote-control tank in the ceilings to pull wires. To the ten-year-old me, it seemed like heaven. In addition to his regular job, Papaw had a series of side businesses such as designing, fabricating, and installing an automated barrel washing line for a local barrel company, rehabbing houses for profit, and even helping start a highly successful machine shop that is still in business today. Papaw had been married once before he married Granny, but details of that marriage were never mentioned to me as a child. In my research, I was able to find her name and the dates of the marriage, but as it was brief and lacking anything of note, I will respect the previous silence on the subject.

If there was one overall quality Papaw had that overshadowed all others, it was that he was patient. I'm not just saying that he didn't mind waiting for the dentist-patient; I mean that he had the patience of a saint. Papaw would endure any amount of abuse, mistreatment, neglect, or selfishness someone could throw his way. This was doubly true if the anger wasn't genuine in its aim at him. That is to say, if Granny was mad or upset at something my mother did and she took her anger out on him, he would sit there and take it, absorbing every volley and blow, knowing that she was really angry at something else. Papaw used and perhaps overused this skill during his life, constantly absorbing and patiently accepting whatever came his way, deserved or not. This trait of patience, its close cousin perseverance, and generosity served as the defining characteristics of his life.

Looking back on things, I can't help but feel some degree of sympathy or admiration for him getting married to Granny. Granny was just getting out of an abusive second marriage that had taken a toll on her and her children. Financially crippled from yet another terrible marriage and other setbacks, Granny faced a very uncertain future. She had three teens who were unruly, quarrelsome, and just old enough not to want input from any adults. Papaw entered into this arrangement with open eyes and arms and began financially providing for the family. He purchased a house for his new family in Burlington, KY, in June of 1976, two months before their official marriage in August of 1976. The house was a cute, wood-framed, white cape cod. It had three bedrooms and a garage, enough room for the kids to have their own space. There was a little work to be done, but he remodeled every room over the next twenty years. That was now his home and his family's home, the first step in the slow process of making a life and family with Granny and her kids. Regardless of how the marriage started over time, it grew and developed into a true family for all of the right reasons. The love that existed between Russell and Gloria was real and very deep; he loved all of her children as his own and was never hesitant in sharing that love with others.

One thing I hadn't previously detailed was that Granny had experienced a series of health setbacks. Those setbacks first manifested when she was at work in the 1960s, shortly after the birth of her children. Granny had trained as a nurse at St. Elizabeth Hospital in Northern KY. After graduation, she worked her way up to charge nurse. In talking to other nurses who worked with her over the years, it is a near-universal sentiment she was a nurse's nurse. There was nothing she was more suited for in this world than to be a nurse. Years later, I heard similar sentiments about my mother and her career. I feel that the intense desire to help and heal is part of them—it could never be stripped away if you were to maintain the person's identity.

Granny's identity was stripped away while working as a charge nurse, and she began to experience chest pains. Luckily, she was in the right place. By the end of the week, she was the recipient of one of the first open-heart bypasses ever performed, a very new procedure for that time. While the surgery successfully saved the young Mom's life, the damage had already been done to the heart and would hound her for the rest of her life. Her career as a nurse was effectively over as she could no longer put in the long hours she had become accustomed to. By the summer of 1981, the end of her career would be official, and she would be declared disabled and retire. The loss of her career was a tough blow for her as it had always been a part of her identity, so much so that when she was buried, it was with a neat and properly folded nurse's cap placed on her gray hair.

To understand how challenging the loss of Granny's nursing career was for her, you need to know how hard she had fought to have that career in the first place. Granny met her first husband—a fellow nursing student, during her studies. Falling in love and becoming pregnant soon followed. Granny then struggled to support and juggle her schooling while keeping a growing family. That task of supporting a family became nearly impossible when her first husband left to buy a pack of cigarettes and never returned, just as the last child was born. It was only with the help of her sister that she was able to graduate from nursing school. Hearing stories about that time when I was growing up, I got the following impression: the family was a communal group of six teenage siblings and cousins tag-teamed by two working and one student parent. Anna (Granny's sister), her husband Blackie, and a healthy dose of free-range freedom that only the '70s could afford were what made Granny's graduation possible.

Following the initial heart attack, Granny would have two more bypasses and at least one stent in her lifetime. This episodic journey of hospitalizations would punctuate nearly every part of her life. It controlled what kind of food she ate, what medicine she was on, and what cardiologist or doctor she had to see that day. Beyond having a practical effect on her life, her health concerns also served a second, more ethereal role. The problem for Granny's health and the possible ramifications of upsetting her became an absolute force. While there was inevitably a certain amount of truth to the concern, it wasn't long until the threat of upsetting her became a real currency in the house; this was something I would learn much more about as time went on.

I left off the last chapter with me showing up at my grandparents' house following the stabbing of my dad. In many ways, my arrival back home was a homecoming. I had previously lived there with my Mom a short time after my birth. Although I have no recollection of this previous stay, I can't help but also remember my return feeling positive. Maybe I was finally relieved to be secure—I'm not sure- but ultimately, this trip to Granny's was my homecoming. Looking back many years later, I have a distinct perspective on that time in my life. This includes knowledge of events and circumstances that couldn't have been known or incorporated by a four-year-old. The facts were too harsh and painful ever openly to share. Like so many things in life, my coming back to the house wasn't as simple as it may have seemed. As it turned out, I had already lived an entire lifetime in that house before. The remnants of the previous life were something that hung in the air like a cloud of vapor that you couldn't quite get away from. It was everywhere you looked—a nick-nack on the mantel, a tiny picture on the wall, a box in the closet full of childlike trinkets. As a child, I never could understand it and be almost undoubtedly oblivious to its existence. The only evidence was tiny reverberations, like when Granny would call me Billie or when I would find a Hot-Wheel hidden in the back of a drawer that wasn't mine.

Billie Wayne White was the youngest of three children. By all accounts, he was a fantastic person. Known by his nickname Doodle, he made people smile everywhere he went. A high school football player and popular Billie was a man about town. Ever the charmer, he even took me on my very first trip to the county fair. Hearing his version of events, it was to make sure I wasn't stuck in the house, but to hear others tell the story; I was the bait he used to attract even more girls. What girl doesn't like the idea of a tall, handsome, football-playing charmer pushing a stroller with an equally cute blond-haired, blue-eyed charmer like me. I imagine we were quite the pair. While I don't remember the trip, I am told it was not without some controversy. It is possible my Mom was not made aware of the full scope of his plans for me that hot August night when he agreed to watch me. Either way, I'm glad he took me.

A few days later, Billie died in a car wreck on August 11th, 1981; he was eighteen years old. After work, he hung out with two other friends and headed to the local arcade. When it came time to pile into the car, the boys sniped and wrestled over who got to ride shotgun, with Billie ultimately winning. Conversation in the car had been about what was next in their lives as they had all just graduated. One of the boys—the driver—had recently enrolled in the local vocational program and had convinced Billie he should also enroll in the electronics program at the same school. Ever the tinkerer, this was perfect for Billie. Just seconds later, as they made a lazy left turn towards the arcade, everything when blank.

Billie was killed two miles from his home while riding in the front passenger seat of his friend's car. They were making a left turn when a motorcycle impacted the vehicle on the passenger side door. Billie was killed instantly. The motorcycle rider had run from the police with his lights turned off. He was likely traveling at nearly 130 MPH at the time of impact. The other passengers were injured but survived. At that speed, to say something was instant is perfectly accurate. There would have been about one-hundredth of a second between the bike impacting the door and it traveling the additional eighteen inches to impact into Billie sitting inside the car. In one-hundredth of a second, so many lives changed forever that night.

When I say the night I returned to the house was a homecoming, I am not saying that from my perspective as a child. It was indeed a homecoming for Granny and Papaw—their son was back. I looked like him, acted like him, and over time I would be told I even sounded like him. That night, I found myself back in their home by fate or circumstance, partially as myself but partially as a proxy for Billie. There were reminders everywhere in the house. Pictures of him on the walls, art projects from his school days, his toys hidden just out of sight. I was a replacement son, but I was also the baby replacement son. Papaw never had his own kids, and he hadn't met Billie until he was a teenager (13). I was, in fact, better than a replacement—I was almost just like the real thing. As you can imagine, this dynamic, while whimsical in concept, isn't healthy or practical in execution. My time as the replacement son was fraught with overindulgence of my every whim. There was overprotection combined with accelerated maturity and independence. This unreasonable overprotection and overindulgence concept can be summed up with a single event.

Much like Billie was very mechanically-inclined, I always took apart my toys or built new inventions in the garage. As I got older, I became a lover of speed. All things fast, loud, and dangerous were my desires. Naturally, every young boy knows what will scratch that itch—a dirt bike. I asked and pleaded. Papaw even took me to the local Honda shop, where I tried on a few for size. When it came time to buy the bike, Papaw quickly ushered me out. I protested and cried as any spoiled kid would do. When we got home, he told me he would talk to Granny and not bring it up as it might upset her (see what she did there). Later that night, ignoring Papaw's advice, I asked Granny if I could have a motorcycle; she said no, they were dangerous. Granny said Billie was killed by a motorcycle, and they were dangerous, adding she couldn't handle anything happening to me. At the time, I didn't have the accident details that I have now. I accepted the decision in my ten-year-old mind as based on fact. I moped around for days, making my displeasure known to anyone who would hear my petition. Later that week, Papaw took me back to the Honda shop and bought me a 110

ATC. The smaller ATC 70 would have been a better fit at that time, but who cares? I'd grow into it right. While it wasn't a dirt bike, it was close. On the way home, the reality suddenly hit me: Granny would be mad. Was she going to get upset? Was her getting upset going to make her need some of her nitro pills—or worse, would it mean she had to go to the hospital again? As we pulled into the driveway, I began to cry and did not know what to do. I looked up, and Granny was outside, ready to look at my new toy. I was confused, but seeing that there were no negative repercussions suddenly allowed me to resume my role as a boy. As an adult, I have a few issues with how this all played out:

1. While benefiting from a good income, was it reasonable to buy a young boy who had half an acre to ride a brand-new ATV? This also completely ignores the fact my pouting and moping were being rewarded.

2. Did anyone notice while Granny was crushing my dream of being a dirt bike owner, she was making it about what she would do if something happened to me. The essence was her saying it was my responsibility not to get hurt as that would hurt her.

3. Big red flag here; The 110ATC, a three-wheeler, is perhaps the single most dangerous power sports vehicle sold in America. Very soon after I got mine, they were banned and went the way of the lawn dart and uranium-filled chemistry set. This was, in fact, much less safe than a dirt bike.

4. The fear of maybe hurting my Granny by upsetting her was so intense it destroyed my natural childish joy of getting a new three-wheeler. Don't win the lottery, kids, because the taxes will make you wish you'd never even won it.

5. The grand finally—Billie wasn't riding a motorcycle when he died. The car he was in was hit by one. Luckily, he wasn't hit by another car, or it would have killed everyone else in the car, and I would have never been able to have my own car. Later in life, I found out that when he died, he owned a nice Yamaha and that my Granny's hatred for motorcycles led her to

get rid of it after his death. Talk about holding a grudge—that woman forsook an entire mode of transportation because of one idiot who carelessly used one with truly grave consequences.

Dirt bikes, Granny guilt, and replacement son syndrome weren't the only perils of living with my grandparents. Granny and Papaw always tried to shield me from the chaos of my Mom. They always made it easy for her to come to see me and take me places. Sometimes a little too easy. I still remember going swimming with my Mom and having the pool manager call my grandparents to get me by the end of the day because my Mom was passed out drunk in the grass. In the end, I began to adapt and cope with simple chaos like that. It eventually became a part of who I was and affected my behaviors. I am a precise planner that insists on details, itineraries, contact numbers, and addresses when I travel. I learned this as a survival trait. If I went somewhere with my Mom, I needed to make sure I could always call Papaw to come to get me if things got weird. It wasn't enough to know how to reach him; I also needed to know where I was so I could direct him to me. That got me to memorize street signs, landmarks, and addresses. To this day, I can travel most of the county I grew up in and point out landmarks, not based on what they are, but rather based on the one time something wrong happened at that place. It was also at that time I started to develop my spidey sense. I use that term because I don't know what else to call my ability to determine the safety of a given situation or person intellectually. I had been involved with my fair share of nefarious activities and had some bad run-ins with perverts, creeps, thieves, and worse. I learned through necessity how to identify them and steer clear. This trait still comes in handy to this day. You would be surprised how often corporate executives set off the same alarms as the perverts at the biker bars.

There were always risks when going somewhere with my Mom, as you might expect. Sometimes I wonder why Granny and Papaw ever let me go. What might surprise you more is that sometimes the danger would come to me. As my Mom dealt with her issues over the years, a few patterns began to emerge. There was a component related to alcohol and drugs. Deep-seated anger and rage were consistently below the surface, ready to be triggered. Those could be accounted for and managed. The fundamental dangerous element that couldn't be mitigated was the calendar. I have had the privilege to see how other people deal with grief in the thirty-plus years since being a child. Some have funerals that end in giant parties, while others are content with a quiet potluck dinner. I even know one family that memorialized a relative's passing with planned excess drinking—not the kind of fire I would play with, but to each his own. While most people treat the initial wake as the big event—and perhaps the corresponding birthday and anniversary of the death—with some reverence and remembrance, it is likely that the significance of these dates dim over time. That is not to say the dates ever lose their relevance or importance, but just that each year the grieving processes get a little easier, and people are better prepared to proceed with life.

That's most people. Unfortunately for my family, they keep track of that shit like some kind of macabre date book with the passing of every aunt, uncle, and acquaintance marked. This is compounded by the fact Billie was so young when he died. Of course, Granny had flowers placed on his birthday each year in the shape of the numbers. Of course, she would take a memorial trip to see his grave every week. That was expected; that wasn't strange. Over the years, I began to notice that the amount of grief expressed by my Mom seemed to grow each year and at each milestone. This growing grief and sorrow exploded from my Mom on or about what would have been Billie's twenty-first birthday.

Around dark—or just after—there was a knock on the door. Papaw answered the door and stepped outside, and what followed was some minor commotion and shuffling sounds. It was my Mom—more correctly, it was someone bringing my Mom back to the house. She was drunk and acting like a fool.

She had been staying with us for a few weeks, but she was rarely seen or heard by me. I believe she was either working nights as a nurse or as a server—perhaps both. By the time she got home, I was usually already in bed. Not tonight. This night I was wide awake, primed to watch Dallas or Magnum PI with Granny—you know, old people shit. With the assistance of whoever brought her home, Papaw managed to get her upstairs and into bed. About forty-five minutes later, I started to hear crying and screaming. Amazingly, this in itself wasn't particularly alarming to me. Granny went up to confront and ultimately yell at her for being out and getting so drunk. After that first round, it was time for me to go to bed, which would have been just before the news.

As I was going to bed, I could see Granny talking to Papaw; she was agitated and had a big, red scratch on her face. I didn't think much of it at the time—it's almost as if my time away from the front lines had started to make me a little soft. As I lay in bed, I started hearing stuff break. Those sounds weren't small breaks like you got from dropping a plate. They were big breaks. I could hear plastic and glass crunch. Even at that age, I knew what it was that had broken. My Mom had a yellow and white-lighted makeup mirror. One side was magnified, and the other was plain. I remember as a kid watching her spend hours getting ready in front of it, hot curlers in her hair, a cigarette in one hand, and mascara in the other. There was something about the brittleness of the plastic, the tinniness of the hollow body combined with the glass breaking that gave it away.

I started hearing more thumps and bangs. It sounded as if the whole house was shaking. Pictures rattled on the wall. Dishes rattled in the cabinets. There was an unending litany of crashes and booms. I didn't dare get any closer than the bottom of the steps. From that vantage point, I could see the debris scattered in the hall at the top of the steps. I knew I was right; it was the mirror she had broken. Papaw made his way upstairs in an effort to calm her down, but his presence only served to make things worse. He was too big of a teddy bear to restrain her, so he was left with only defensive moves to protect his eyes and face from her claw-like fingernails. I sat there in shock, peaking around the doorway at the bottom of the steps, watching this happen. This hulk of a man with the biggest hands I had ever seen was driven back by a 120-pound woman.

I realized things might have been getting a little out of hand. It was about that time the screaming started. First, it was shouts and screams that were high-pitched and shrill. The initial sounds weren't unlike what you would hear in a classic horror movie. But then came the more profound, visceral sounds—like a cougar's roar mixed with a deep, billowy breath to finish it off. You could hear her vocal cords cracking as she screamed her anger away. Next came the ripping and tearing. At first, it was a relief to listen to the volume decrease, but that was a false sense of calm; she moved to another mode. She started tearing every piece of fabric in that room. Strip by strip, piece by piece. The sheets, the curtains, clothes, the pillows, even the mattress. As the cadence of the destruction slowed, the sounds of crashing and breaking became methodical. My Mom had moved on to another phase of destruction—the systematic phase. She began breaking one-by-one every single picture and nick-nack in that room. I couldn't see the actual events as I was still hiding at the bottom of the steps, but every detail was clear and vivid. I was hearing in color, my brain instantly connecting the crash or crack to an object or surface. Once again, Granny tried to stop her; that is when I started to get scared.

I had previously been conditioned not to make Granny angry or upset as it could hurt her heart, and she could get sick or die. I saw Granny madder than I would ever see her in my life. She was red in the face and screaming at my Mom. My instinct was that Granny knew what was upsetting my Mom—either by reckoning or possibly through actually hearing what my Mom was screaming—but I still had no idea. My Mom pushed Granny, and they got into a hair-pulling match. Little did Granny know my Mom was the world champion at hair pulling. I had watched her hone her skills at honky-talks and biker bars through the years. I learned how this was going to end. My Mom let go of Granny as she pushed her out the door. You could hear the door slam shut, but there wasn't a reverberation or secondary vibration; it was just the single thud you might expect if someone fell against the door just as it closed.

Granny was out of breath. Papaw tried to attend to Granny, shush me away, and get into the room simultaneously. In the minutes that followed, he called the cops and told them what had happened while Granny was in the kitchen icing her face with a cold towel, trying to calm down. I don't remember her pulling out the nitro pills at that time, but if there ever was a time, it was then. By my count, it was the end of round two, with the first two rounds going squarely in my Mom's favor. She had begun talking—or chanting—with a melodic cadence to what she was saying. It wasn't calming but certainly didn't have the chilling effect of the primal screams. Our house was exactly two blocks from the police station, so I noticed blue lights outside within minutes. At that time, the local police used silver cars with blue light-bars. Their uniforms were gray with a black stripe down the sides of the pants and on the shoulders. They wore traditional wide-brimmed campaign hats, and at that time of year, they were wearing short sleeves. Papaw met them at the door, and pretty quickly, they could hear her upstairs and started the negotiation. I say negotiation only in jest—it was a quick set of commands rebuffed promptly with my Mom's personal brand of expletives and vitriol. Some of the only words I remember from that night involve her exchange with the cops as they stood at the bottom of the stairs.

As a side note, it is essential to know my Mom—along with most of the family—laid much, if not all, of the blame on the police for the events on the night of Billie's death. They blamed the police more than they did the motorcycle rider or even the motorcycle. It had always been the family's contention that the high-speed chase wasn't necessary and was reckless given the speed, lack of lights, and amount of traffic. As you will find in a later chapter, I am somewhat agnostic on high-speed chases.

But rest assured, as far as my Mom was concerned, the officer yelling orders to her had been the same one that had killed her brother.

The officers' arguments did not compel my Mom, nor were they likely to retreat, considering the threats she threw their way. The officers, sensing the escalating nature of the confrontation and the tactical disadvantage they faced working uphill on a very steep and narrow set of stairs, consulted with Papaw and developed a plan. They made it clear they would try not to damage anything, but they had to take her. You could hear more glass breaking; it wasn't a mirror but a window. Granny rushed to the front of the house to see if she had climbed out. Thankfully she had just broken the window, not tried to escape. The assault was about to begin, and I kept a low profile around the corner in the kitchen. The officers forced open the door. The door cracked and splinted with the sound of cheap plywood despite it being much more robust. My Mom had piled debris against the door, keeping it from opening fully. Papaw tried to hold it open as the officers tackled and restrained her. But just like when you trap a wild raccoon, you have to be prepared for a full-effort fight. Mom was no different. The cops had her hands restrained and in cuffs, but she was still fighting, hair, spit, and blood spraying like a fountain. As the officers crested the top of the steps, one in front and one in the back, she made her last stand. Like an alligator in a death roll, she twisted and squirmed. Fueled by adrenaline and who knows what else, she kicked her legs up and braced against the narrow hallway walls. I could see with precise detail that she flailed and contorted so much that her feet walked along with the stairwell's ceiling. Moments later, the entire churning mass of officers and mother alike slid down the stairs. I got partially trapped under the pile as Papaw came down from behind and helped the officers up while still holding her.

I don't know if every last ounce of her adrenaline was spent or if she just knew she was defeated, but the fight began to leave her body. What were tears of rage and visceral screams turned into sobbing and almost childlike pleading? The officers took her outside to the car. I didn't see her get placed into the car, but I heard the false crescendo in the house lull the two officers into complacency. They had to tame yet another tiger to get her into the car. Round three—Boone County Police Department with a KO. The officers spent another twenty to thirty minutes getting statements and information at the house. At least one of the officers either knew my grandparents or my Mom as he was engaging in an excessively human way—a courtesy not often extended to strangers by police, especially in light of the circumstances. One of the officers addressed me in a soft, caring voice and reassured me that my Mom would be alright and they were going to take her to the hospital to get help.

My Mom was taken to a behavioral health unit, where she spent several days. She had been seriously distraught over Billie's birthday, and given that it was his twenty-first, she likely partook in excessive alcohol. That excess consumption combined with the fact she was staying in his old room was a perfect storm. That was all on top of the inadequacies she must have felt like a mother who was a guest in her own son's home. It was just too much for her to handle that day. It might have been too much for anyone, as they were some pretty significant burdens only made worse when you added addiction and drugs to the mix. That was the last time I remember Mom spending the night at my grandparents. The room in which my Mom so completely and thoroughly destroyed was repaired and turned into my room. I was even allowed to pick out a new bedspread and sheets from the JC Penney catalog—maybe it was some kind of perverse consultation prize for surviving the freak-out. Everyone did their best to act as if that night never happened, but it's certainly has earned a spot next to the other BIG memories in my book.

That night, I learned there was no such thing as truly safe, only danger adjacent. No matter how far I came or how different things were, I knew there was always a little danger just around the corner. It can change instantly, no matter how secure or safe you think something is.

Chapter 4

CRAZY: Football School and Trouble

Growing up, I always had a lot of energy; it didn't matter how busy I was; I needed more to do. I attribute that to being one of the only kids who lived within the two - three-mile radius I was allowed to roam. Burlington was a great small town, but it was a small town. A quick view of Google Earth shows precisely forty-nine houses within my approved range. As you are aware, the untimely murder of my uncle by a possessed and self-aware motorcycle ten years prior weighed heavy on my family. This fear for my survival created a situation that resulted in me being constrained to a territory that included only residential surface streets with sidewalks that didn't require crossing any main roads despite there being crosswalks and stoplights.

I was limited by a lack of sidewalks and a lumber yard to the north. The southern limit was KY 18, a busy two-lane road with only two stoplights and two off-limited sets of crosswalks. To the east was the local elementary school, of which I had full reign of the playground but couldn't use the walking trails connecting it to the adjacent apartments until many years later. Finally, I was bound by the remnants of an older neighborhood containing five or six houses to the west. The neighborhood either came and went before my time or perhaps never fully materialized despite a tidy grid pattern of streets and a micro-sized park.

I knew of at least five sets of grandparents of kids my age and precisely one other kid in those forty-nine houses. This other kid must have been a bubble boy because I don't think I ever saw him outside and was consistently rebuffed when I would knock on his door. That changed around fourth grade when three new kids moved in and expanded further in fifth grade when I got my territory extended to include a new subdivision to the south and the apartment complex in the east. Using trails versus roads, I leveraged this additional territory, assuaging fears I would be run over or kidnapped.

The town itself was quaint and included at least five churches, three daycares, the courthouse, a diner, a gas station, a hardware store/seed shop, two barbershops, and an auto parts store. Looking back on things, I have always wondered why we had so many churches but only one restaurant that included a bar, making it off-limits by doctrine to the congregants of each of the five churches. It would seem someone missed an opportunity there.

Suffice to say, Burlington was the quintessential 1950's small town in America. The only problem was this was the 80s, and instead of sock hops and cap guns, we had Nintendo and MTV. Since I didn't have video games or cable TV, my days were spent riding my bike, surveying my range like a wild lion checking my territory. Instead of playing, I was looking for moving trucks, hoping some new kids would be moving in, or as a consolation prize, find a sign of grandkids that may have been visiting grandparents in the area. On a typical day, I may have made ten to fifteen laps of the neighborhood. I knew which sections of lifted and broken sidewalks I could jump with my bike. I knew what yards I could cut through and which ones I couldn't. I even knew how to get a drink of ice-cold water and a blast of air conditioning in the middle of the summer when the humidity was thick, and the sun was high. Coincidently, after living in three other states in the thirty years since, I now live less than ten miles from Burlington. I occasionally visit, and not much has changed. The hardware store is now a restaurant, but

I can still see the remnants of the old layout inside—I can tell where the seeds were and the room that held the big bins full of nails and bolts. The gas station is gone (technically moved and restored a few blocks away), and a few new restaurants are filling out previously abandoned houses. Overall, not much has changed. My childhood home is essentially unchanged, with only the addition of a fence in the backyard after thirty years. I can still see the trees in the front yard that started as live Christmas trees. Papaw had a tradition of buying live Christmas trees, roots, and all. Every year we drug the monsters inside, and after Christmas, we pulled them back out and planted them in the front yard. It's hard to describe exactly how it feels to see a pine tree in front of a house that you remember as your actual Christmas tree as a child.

The world's coldest and best flowing water fountain exists right where I left it thirty years ago. I can still remember the double doors opening, letting the cold air-conditioned air spill out, the feeling of the frigid air on my sweaty sun-kissed skin. The water coming out of the fountain was almost too cold, the kind of cold that would hurt your teeth if you didn't drink it right. I have traveled the world and never encountered a water fountain like this one. The last time I was in the area, I stopped in and tested it. You will be happy to know the water fountain is just as cold as ever and available every weekday at the old—but not too old—Boone County Courthouse.

I have to admit, part of me was scared to try the water fountain again; what if it wasn't as good as I remembered? Is it possible it broke, and they replaced it or changed the settings? What if it was exactly as it had been when I was a kid, but now it wasn't as exceptional when objectively measured against others? That's the funny thing about memories—sometimes they need a little fact-checking, and sometimes you have to wonder if they have changed or how you measure them has changed.

Thinking of memories and Burlington, another synchronicity comes to mind. I was six or seven years old and ready to head into first grade. I spent my days as a rambunctious boy tearing around the neighborhood on my bike while screaming like a banshee. I had just gotten to the milestone in every free-range kid's life where it had become commonplace to be locked out of the house—or, more accurately, the screen door. Granny would grow tired of my antics, and it was time I went and bothered someone else with my questions and jabbering. That was also the summer just before Papaw retired. That meant I still had to not so patiently wait for him to get home each day before my best friend and I could take a walk around the neighborhood or start working on some project or invention in the garage. It wasn't unheard of for me to sit and wait in the front yard under a shady tree, looking for his pickup to pull down the street. Unfortunately, I couldn't inherit his patience due to the lack of blood relations. Still, he somehow understood this and always did his best to accommodate my impatience. This despite having just worked an entire shift and navigating traffic both ways.

One day in late summer, Papaw pulled into the driveway, and he seemed a little more excited to see me than usual. He said let's go for a walk. I rode my bike, never wanting to walk, and he walked behind me. We headed straight to the elementary school. As it was late summer and school was still on break, I didn't expect there to be much activity. To my surprise, there were kids everywhere. There were girls lined up at cheer leading practice down the sidewalk on the side of the school—this was pretty common, and no need for excitement. Something less expected was the line of boys—some as young as me and many that were a bit older—next to an old blue van. While you could be forgiven for assuming the worst based on some of the previous stories in this book, this will not be one of those stories. The boys were lined up getting football equipment. There were piles of helmets and shoulder pads. Separate bags were lined up down the sidewalk edge filled with pants and jerseys. At that point, what I was seeing hadn't quite hit me. I don't even know if I knew what peewee football was, much less that I could play it using a real uniform with pads and all. You have to remember, my neighborhood peer group at the time consisted of Ms.

Ferguson, who was born during the Lincoln administration.

After the commotion died down, Papaw and I walked up to the coach, and he asked me how old I was. I replied with six, which was a bit young for full-contact peewee football, especially considering the oldest kids in my same division would be four grades ahead of me. Papaw and Coach Napier went back and forth a little, and they agreed I could try on one condition. I was allowed to give it a shot with the understanding if it was too tough this year and I didn't want to play because the kids were too rough, I had to give it another shot the following year once I got a little older. This was a perfectly reasonable and practical position for the coach to take. He didn't want the chubby/hyper kid to completely askew football forever after a few nasty hits as a six-year-old—he was thinking ahead.

I look back on this as the first opportunity I had as a human to truly make my own decision about something. The coach talked to me and laid out the terms of the deal directly to me. He didn't look to Papaw for the answer; he looked at me. He had expressed the terms, shared the risk, and had given me reasonable expectations if I were to accept the deal. By any measure or arbitration, that was a fair deal. It was also clear if I accepted that deal, I would be bound by it. It wasn't Papaw's deal, it was mine, and if it didn't work out this year, I would have to be right back there the next year doing it all over again. I took a second to pause and think about it. I looked down at my feet; I was wearing a pair of flip-flops. I looked back up and asked Coach Napier if I could go back to my house to get my shoes. He asked how far away it was, and I said it was just a block away. The coach said if you can get back in eight minutes, you can, but he didn't tolerate being late, and if I wasn't on time, I had to wait until the next day to start. The distance between that van and my front door was 1,164 ft. Never in the history of Burlington had a six-year-old made the trip to and from in less time. Running into the house, I excitedly told Granny I had to get shoes so I could play football and was back out the door just as fast. I made it back in time to get my equipment on, and from that day on, I was a football player.

To this day, I don't know if Papaw knew beforehand there was a football team I could join or if it had just been a happy coincidence. Either way, I am grateful he was willing and able to help me take those first steps. When I played for the Blackhawks my first year, I was issued the number - sixty-four. It was a simple, black jersey with two large bright yellow numbers on the chest and the back, nothing more, nothing less. Over the years, I would have many different jerseys and numbers, but I will never forget that first one. I was special more than any other. Fast forward twenty-four years, and I helped my oldest son take those very same first steps. He played for the same team, with the same coach, and wore the same jersey. Not just the same number, the actual same jersey. He only played one year, and I kept the jersey at the end of the season. I figured being able to share that connection with him was genuinely precious and worth whatever fee I paid for not returning it. Football won't mean the same thing for him as it did for me, and I am grateful. For it to mean the same thing to him, he would have had to of walked a mile in my shoes first, and I wouldn't wish that on anyone, especially my son.

The practice was four days a week in the evening before school started. In the fall, it switched to three days a week. I lacked one thing for all of my enthusiasm and hubris—fitness. I was athletic enough as I loved to climb trees and ride my bike, but I was also what is most accurately described as a "good eater." I had always been sickly when I lived with my mom, and I suspect that led to a slight overfeeding once I was with Granny. There wasn't a dinner that went by that didn't finish with a glass dish full of Jell-O or pudding. This, combined with a naturally filling southern diet of fried potatoes, cornbread, and bacon, meant I was a little behind the curve when football started.

At the first practice, I was dead last when we ran around the field in a group. My thighs were chaffing, I was hot and sweaty, and the grass made me itch. Things weren't looking good for my football career on day one. Over the following few practices, things got a little better. I never got to be a fast kid and was always one of the last two or three across the line at the end of the run, but at least I could finish the run. After calisthenics, the fun started. The other kids were easily distracted and didn't pay much attention. Unlike them, I was focused like a laser. Hell, I was simply happy to have something to do during the day. I learned the positions and some of the basic plays. This, along with an understanding of the basic rules, helped me catch up quickly.

Once I had the basics down, I could unleash my secret weapon. My secret weapon was the kind of anger, hatred, and pure aggression that could only come from enduring the most severe beatings and experiencing firsthand some of the most fucked-up stuff as part of your everyday existence. The closest parallel I have ever been able to draw for people is when you hear the stories about child soldiers in war-torn countries. The kids that watched their mom's rapes, their dad's get stabbed. The kids have been betrayed and taken advantage of by nearly every person who has authority over them. Check, check, and check; I was the living embodiment of that. I was the fat, American equivalent of a blood-thirsty child soldier. It only took a few days before I became comfortable with the coaches and hit the other kids hard. At first, I was afraid that I would get in trouble. I assumed the other kids knew something I didn't about the rules, and since they weren't hitting me hard, I shouldn't hit them hard. It never occurred to me what I considered pain and what others considered pain may not have been the same things. I also didn't grasp the power that fear could wield. Up until that point, I had always been on the receiving end of fear. I knew what it was like to fear something terrible happening to me in retaliation for what I did, but no one had ever feared me or what I could do.

As it turns out, all six or seven-year-old boys have a spidey sense, and those kids could tell I was to be feared. They didn't know why or how, and they didn't need to—they simply knew they didn't want to hit me hard out of fear I would take their head off in retaliation. By the end of the first week, they had to take me away from the kids my age and place me with the older kids. In a week, I had gone from the kid who had to make a special deal because he might not have been able to cut it to one of the most physically dangerous kids in my division.

Sensing I needed some sort of reality check, one of the assistant coaches made a misguided attempt at putting me in my place. We were doing some fumble drill, and he had arranged for the whole team to pile on top of me when it was my turn. Not knowing any better, I happily jumped on the ball, covering it as the ball sat just below my sternum, pressing into my belly. If you've played football any time, you know what happens next. As each kid jumped and piled on me, the ball was shoved deeper and deeper into my guts. The pain was immense, and my breath was taken away. I struggled to breathe and gasped for breath. I had been defeated.

At that point, I went into full survival mode. Not the eight-year-old I-fell-off-my-bike-and-I-have-an-owie mode, but my-paw-is-stuck-in-a-steel-trap-and-it's-time-to-gnaw-it-off mode. My gasp for air turned into the deep, visceral, primal screams that I had learned from my mom the summer before. I began to fight and scream, ultimately standing up with the entire group trying to hold me down. Much like you hear stories of a mother lifting a Volkswagen off her child, at that moment, I was capable of superhuman strength. That wasn't normal or repeatable but was merely the inevitable outcome of the panic and adrenaline released because I was in genuine danger and pain. When I got free, I finally let out a laugh, and with all the bravado I could muster, I asked, "if that was all they had?" From that moment on, I had a nickname. It was more than that, though; it became an identity. It wouldn't be until decades later that I understood how powerful that nickname truly was. How merely being called by the name could simultaneously elicit feelings of pride and shame. How a single, simple word—nutty—could become a burden, I felt I could never get away from it. It wasn't a stretch to say many people felt the nickname was somehow legitimate and was a real diagnosis or condition. Teachers and principals would make assumptions based on it—not knowing me from Adam, simply acting based on an "insane" rumor they had heard. Countless times I would find myself in a "kooky," surreal third-party moment when people would be talking about me and referring to me by my nickname without realizing I was the one they were talking about. If you take it a step further and consider my history and circumstances, I was stripped of my identity a second time. The first time was when the lines between who Billie had been and who I was becoming had been blurred, and now it was happening again through a series of events. However, the undertones and implications weren't as innocuous, and real harm was done.

It is essential, of course, to be clear that I am writing these statements about how I feel about it now. I am using adult reasoning and adult experience. I would be lying if I didn't tell you there were parts of that nickname I loved. Having a "deranged" handle like that was the closest a kid could ever come to being famous. I was the first to use it to my advantage anytime I could. By the time I was twelve or thirteen, I was genuinely infamous among my peer group. To this very day, among a subset of adults of a certain age in Boone County, the simple mentioning of the name will get you a reaction; it won't always be a good reaction, but it will be a reaction nonetheless. There were "wacky" rumors—some partially true and some utterly outlandish. As a stupid kid, I never started any of the rumors, but I never denied them either. I hid behind the false bravado of "let people think what they want; I know who I am." That would have been a great approach—unfortunately, it wasn't practical. To pull off that sort of recovery would have taken an emotional maturity I probably don't have today, much less when I was in middle and high school. With that nickname and its inevitable impact, I had somehow stumbled on adult concepts of promotion and meeting expectations that only PT Barnum would fully be able to grasp.

Ultimately, I would play football for the next ten years. At every level possible, I played up to the next highest group. When I was a Peewee, I moved up to midget. When I was in eighth grade, I played high school. When I was a first-year student, I played varsity, and the last summer I played, I practiced with the college players at various camps and workshops. I was never the biggest or the strongest but was instead one of the smartest, and I played with an unequaled level of heart. I also wasn't above using a little intimidation afforded to me by my nickname. At some point, the blending of reality and persona became unhealthy. A "silly" nickname that had its roots in a single play in practice evolved into a situation where parents would offer bounties for me to hurt other kids… Think about that for a second. My flexible child-soldier morality and my willingness to do anything to be accepted and loved led to me hurting other children for money. I went from child to mercenary in just two or three easy steps. I will always have to carry a little guilt from what I did to hurt others when I played. It wasn't a competition or just part of the game; it was malicious and intentional. I somehow used football as an excuse or reason to be savage. I would seek retribution for the pain I had endured. I felt better, or somehow avenged, by inflicting it on others, justified in pain affliction for my own needs. Sometimes this afflicting of pain was for profit, sometimes it was for ego, and sometimes to satisfy a primal desire to hurt others because I was hurting.

I also used football to give me purpose and drive. I used it to make myself a better person, and ultimately if it weren't for football, I probably would have never even gone to high school at all. I was happy to have shared football with my son, but it was never hard to decide that it wasn't something I wanted him to participate in long-term.

Modern youth sports are unhealthy and, in my opinion, offer only limited upside and vast potential for downside for their child participants.

Today I despise sports, particularly sports parents, for the reasons I just mentioned. People assume I shy away from sports because I was a nerd or wasn't any good at sports—that's not it.

I despise sports and sports parents because of the physical and emotional power and the detrimental effect they can have on children when even the slightest deviation occurs. The same parents that don't save for their kids' college because they are counting on a scholarship are the first ones ready to pay a monster like me to hurt the competition.

It would be dishonest to say that football didn't play a defining role in my life despite the outcome. It wasn't always a positive definition, but it indeed was defining. I was defined for the first time on a hot August afternoon on a dusty field as I emerged from the pile of child-humanity. I was forever defined as Crazy, and that simple word instantly became my nickname, my new identity. Over the years, that nickname would have different definitions and levels of power over me, but deep down, it always represented something terrible for me. It represented how I was broken, or at least not as expected, just like others in my life had been. I was exactly like some of those who I loved and who I also feared. It was official—everyone could see it, and it was so plain no one even hesitated to use it instead of my name. My name wasn't Justin or Jason, or even Billie or Doodle. It was **CRAZY.**

Justin "CRAZY" White (64) 1987-1997

There was another aspect of my life that was particularly defining, and that was school. When I had started first grade, I probably wasn't the best prepared. I couldn't read yet, and I wasn't much of a skip counter. I'm not sure if this delay was related to me not being exposed to those types of formal concepts earlier, or if maybe when presented with a situation in which I could either be good at counting or I could be good at reading a room and picking the proper adult for help, I liked the later more practical option. Midway through the first grade, reading quickly came to me, and I could count by two, five, ten, etc. I had excelled enough that I was even moved up to the next level of math class for one brief moment- a solitary day. I will never know whether it was my distracting behavior or a teacher's confidence that my placement in their class had been a mistake and I couldn't possibly keep up with the smart kids. I know the next day, I was put right back into the average kid class. To be honest, I don't know if I even understood why I was being moved in the first place. Once I got that tiny hour-long taste of the intelligent class, I was devastated to go back. I was placed in the middling classes for the next several years to the best of my recollection.

It wasn't until fourth grade when I again had been identified by some standardized test as having potential, that I was again given a chance; however, just like the last time, the teacher, Ms. Northcutt had, evaluated me and found me lacking. She had me do a bunch of spelling words—which was my worst subject—and filled out some notes. Coincidently, this is the same teacher who taught me for an entire hour a few years earlier before deciding I couldn't cut it in her advanced math class. I never heard back about the program or the testing company, and it was safe to assume I hadn't met the criteria. The other students didn't think I was exceptional or even moderately intelligent either. I'm not sure if it was because I was fat and a bit of a loaner due to my somewhat limited roaming territory or if there was something else I was lacking—which is entirely possible. Maybe something inside of me just hadn't clicked yet. That was all about to change.

Since I lived close to the school, I walked and didn't need to catch the bus. I could take my time leaving school each day. I would clean chalkboards for teachers, join clubs and groups, pretty much anything. It wasn't that I didn't want to go home; I just didn't have much of a reason to go home. One day after school, they were having tryouts for the academic team. This team was a kid's version of a quiz show or Jeopardy. The use of an electronic buzzer system was the most appealing aspect for me and was almost certainly why I had tried it out. Lowe and behold, it turned out I was rather good at that sort of thing. By the end of the session, I had beat every other kid. The teachers' kids, the gifted class kids, the kids a grade above didn't matter; I just beat them. My only weaknesses were spelling and math.

Spelling has never connected with me, and I wasn't as fast at math as some of the other kids. My awareness of my shortcomings in these two subjects was used to my advantage. I would simply buzz in and get the wrong answer right away. This meant the other team or competitor would have the opportunity for an immediate response versus waiting for the countdown timer to tick away. My strategy was the sooner I could get away from math or spelling, the better my chances were to score points with stuff I did know well. This strategy wasn't always the most popular, but if I had to do it over again today, I would choose the same one.

The academic team was perhaps my first actual success in school academically. The public nature also meant no one could ignore my successes or take them away from me. Getting a good grade on a test was one thing, but a good grade didn't carry much weight unless you walked around like a jerk showing everyone your scores. This is a stark contrast to the academic team. In a match, you're sitting at a table going head-to-head with equals while the audience of parents and teachers are around to see it. More important than the audience was that they always announced the team had won the match the next day during the morning announcements. If you had an awe-inspiring performance, they might even say how many correct answers you had. For a kid in elementary school, it got no better than that.

This success for me also came at a crucial time. As I discussed earlier, a separate part of me started to gain some attention, which wasn't all good. By the end of fifth grade, the drama surrounding my nickname was beginning to affect me, and it was bleeding into aspects well beyond football. I was stuck balancing a Jekyll and Hyde identity. On one side, I was the budding academic who dutifully participated in every club and extracurricular possible. I had climbed up from being underestimated to being an academic star all on my own in a way that my bona fides couldn't be questioned. I also had the darker side to contend with. I had a reputation as aggressive and uncontrollable. I was receiving enormous amounts of attention by giving into my most primal desires, and I was able to embrace that identity without censoring or holding back my behavior. When I played the academic role, I never felt like I truly belonged. I felt I was an impostor, and I had to keep up a particular persona or image to keep fitting in. Furthermore, it was that persona of the academic I wanted the most. In the end, I was able to keep the balancing act going for a few more years, with a few hiccups in between. My first trips to the principal's office were minor, but they grew and grew over time. At one point, I was even leveraging my academic reputation to buoy me out of trouble, but even that couldn't go on forever. By the time I was in high school, I had quit all the extra activities and openly embraced the Hyde identity. It wasn't the one I wanted, but it seemed like that identity had chosen me after so long.

Ultimately, that is what I struggled with the most from the age of six to sixteen. Even as an adult, I don't know that I have accurate and complete answers to how everything evolved. On the one hand, I very much see everyday life with a young man trying to define himself and figure out who he is. Conversely, I see outside influences and forces dragging him to become precisely what he doesn't want to be. The nickname Crazy had an almost magnetic effect—first pulling me towards it and ultimately serving as an aspirational defining characteristic. It became an expectation to be striven towards or lived up to. I had every reason and excuse to be the worst version of myself. No one would have been surprised if I had ended up in jail. In so many ways, that was the expectation. When reconnecting with people who knew me twenty to thirty years ago, one of the most common sentiments is, "I can't believe he's not in jail." And while I understand how someone who only listened to the nickname and rumors might think that outcome was inevitable, I have a challenging time believing it was that simple. I go back to the mere existence of the nickname and second guess myself. Was it just a coincidence, or was it indeed who I was? Have I spent the last thirty years trying to make myself someone I was never supposed to be?

I question myself from time to time by thinking, is it this hard for everyone else? Are the rest of the humans on this earth spending this much time and effort and failing as much as I do when I try to be something that is otherwise so contrary to their nature? Sometimes I get jealous when I see genuinely good people effortlessly being good, embracing their best selves. They aren't questioning who they are or asking why they have seemingly contradictory identities. Instead, they are living their best life and working on giving that little bit extra next time to make things that much better.

In the end, it comes down to this: I am who I am due to the combination of what has happened to me and what I have done, both good and bad. In my crude estimation, I am about thirty-three percent a real live human being, with the rest being residue and muck I carry as trauma and baggage. No matter how well I do as a parent, my kids will inevitably pick up a little of my baggage and trauma along the way. My kids won't even know they are picking it up, and I won't even know I'm giving it to them, but it will happen nonetheless. They will probably be a full seventy-five percent or more real live humans. If they can avoid the hidden traps and find supportive partners that complement their personalities, they may have kids who are ninety-five percent real live humans. These kids will carry only a fraction of the residue of their parents and grandparents. It likely won't be until the following generation that represents my great-grandchildren will all of my trauma and bullshit be washed away, and they can live life without the cloud and smudges leftover from me.

While the day in which the trauma I carry is finally gone from this world is still a long way off, I believe it can happen. I also think erasing that trauma can never happen if I just accept what's easy and do what offers the least resistance. In my life, accepting what is accessible and what provides the least resistance would be accepting I was "CRAZY," just like people said. It would have allowed me to be violent and act without restraint.

I would have made excuses for what I knew to be wrong on the backs of those who had wronged me. I would have said, “what more do you want from me? I’m doing the best with what I have”. That would have been comfortable and easy, but that approach would never allow my great-grandkids to have a chance at not carrying my bullshit forward into the future. The simple fact I can see this as being a truth that is self-evident and clear is the only reassurance I need to know. You can call me “CRAZY” if you want, but all you are doing is driving me further away from what’s comfortable and easy.

Chapter 5

First Date with Sara and the Rest of the Day

In the fall of 1993, we had just moved from old Burlington to a small farm a few miles away. Papaw had retired from P&G a year earlier to spend more time traveling with Granny. I had continued playing football and picked up a few more hobbies along the way. On top of academics, I was now involved with competitive RC car racing, BMX racing, and spending a fair amount of time roller-skating with my new neighbor, Scott. I finally had friends my age and the freedom and resources I needed to flourish.

The farm was small—only about six acres—and was a bit of a work-in-progress. There would need to be some changes to the house, but in true Papaw fashion, and they started before we even moved in. In addition to the taste changes, we had central air conditioning installed to be more comfortable for Granny. She had always suffered in the heat and humidity of a KY summer. The humidity, in particular, always seemed to make her breathing difficult—well, the humidity and the menthol cigarettes she smoked. In addition to the additions to the house, Papaw had a large lake and a barn added. The lake served as both a fishing and swimming hole, and the barn was to store the numerous snowmobiles, four-wheelers, and tractors we had accumulated over the years since the first 3 wheeler.

In many ways, I had finally started to get some normalcy in my life. Through all of my activities and hobbies, I had begun to make friends and connections that we were able to see me as something besides the kid with the Crazy nickname. One of those connections was Darrell; he was someone who was ultimately going to play a much more significant role in my life, but at that point, he also was still just a kid. The beauty about kids—especially new kids—was that they didn't know a lot of my history, which was good as far as I was concerned. This lack of history meant I didn't have expectations to live up to or be burdened by. I had fallen into a rhythm and a balance as I entered sixth grade. I could be free and explore in the summer, bouncing from one adventure to another. I could be the football player in the fall and get the accolades and attention I so craved. By the time winter and spring came around, I could focus on science fairs, academic teams, and school work. As a middle schooler, I had it all figured out.

On the larger family front, things were also rather good. My Mom had generally gotten her shit together and lived in a house that Papaw had rehabbed for her in Burlington. The house was only about four blocks from my old home in Burlington, so it was a leisurely bike ride before we moved. It was still a doable ride if I used trails and shortcuts even after moving. She had a steady job as a nurse and was doing pretty well. Things had improved to the point that I had would occasionally spend the night there and even have my room. My Mom's drama was generally between her and whatever love interest she had or her sister as long as she wasn't drinking much. Later that year, she had started dating Rick, a man she would ultimately marry a few years later.

By Christmas of '93, the first wrinkles of this new chapter would start to show. Granny loved to cook and especially loved to cook southern food. She would insist on making a meal the old-fashioned way. To Granny, the old-fashioned way meant pulling out the deep fryer and electric skillet. This was a ritual I still don't understand; we already had a perfectly good electric stove and pans; why did we need more? She would lay out all of the ingredients: Crisco, cornmeal, and flour. She would cut up the ingredients just right using a knife that, as far as I could tell, was hand-made by George Washington himself. The knife was thin and over-sharpened. The dark, steel blade had two worn wooden scales as handles, and you could barely see the thin hand-hammered rivets holding the handle on. I asked her about the knife one day, and she said it was "her father's," and I don't have any reason to think that wasn't the case. Later, I would ask myself how she got it from her father? Did she steal from him? Was it a knife she had intended for him, so she referred to it as his? Based on her history and the apparent anger towards most men and him in particular, neither would have surprised me.

That night, Granny was making liver and onions—her favorite. As I was not a fan of liver, I would be getting my own piece or two of fried chicken as an alternative. They were deep-fried just like the liver, with each piece a dark golden brown only achievable with years of experience and the perfect combination of cast iron skillet and Crisco. Granny had perfected her tools and technique to achieve perfect results every time. That pan had a seasoning crust any chef would be proud of—thick and shiny and so smooth you could clean it with a paper towel when you were done. I don't suppose that pan had ever seen a single drop of Dawn or a dishwasher. The American Heart Association would not approve of this meal, nor many others served by Granny.

Following that particular meal, something seemed a little off with Granny. She had already been a little off since learning of her father's passing a few weeks before, which increased her uneasiness. I remember the days and weeks leading up to that night, overhearing some discussions between Granny and Papaw. The whisperings were related to wondering if she was starting to have the symptoms of heart failure. She was getting some pains that came and went from time to time, but she wasn't sure of the cause and felt that it might have just been stress with the move and all. Granny was an old pro at the heart game by that point in time. She generally knew what was going on from experience and training as a nurse. She would down nitro pills like Tic-Tacs, occasionally asking me to retrieve the tiny brown bottle from her purse or the shelf by the sink. She wouldn't hesitate to pull out a blood pressure cuff and stethoscope to diagnose further how bad things were. If she had a particular concern based on what she saw or heard, she might even call my Mom in for a second opinion.

Within a few hours, Granny had Papaw take her to the hospital. I was scared. Despite being young, I knew what that could mean. I had been trained to walk on eggshells and avoid making her mad because she was weak. Knowing what was at stake, everyone was sad, even Granny. As she got ready to leave with Papaw, there was an unspoken uneasiness—was this the event we were all trying to avoid for years? I look back at all of the times she had an incident and recall a clear escalation. Something would happen; she would spend a few days, then a few weeks, and eventually a month in the hospital. I asked how long it would be this time—a month more, would she ever come back?

**You may have noticed I have mentioned a few brand names. If you are a family living in Cincinnati and between your grandfather, great-uncles, and great-grandfather you have nearly 200 combined years of service to P&G; your brand loyalty starts to rival blood relations.*

I stayed at the house as usual. I had gone with them in the past, but I would usually run afoul of visiting age requirements or quickly get bored and seek out the vending machines or cafeterias to pass the time. It was easier to leave me at the house, and Papaw would call me later. I patiently waited for Papaw to come home or, God forbid, my Mom to come to get me. While it was never previously discussed or formalized, my overwhelming desire to plan and prepare for worst-case scenarios had already predicted what might come next. Knowing how much Papaw loved Granny and how fiercely loyal and protective of her he would be, I always figured if something was wrong and she was at risk of dying, Papaw would send my Mom or someone else like my uncle Donnie to get me. I knew there was no way he would leave her side even to come to contact me.

I had gone through the scenarios up and down, back and front. I sat on the couch, waiting and wondering what would happen next. At around 10:30, I saw lights in the driveway. It was hard to determine whose car it was; the glass on the door was beveled and engraved, which distorted the shapes. Baited in anticipation, I could just make out the car. It was Papaw. I guess visiting hours were over. Papaw walked in the door with Granny close behind a few moments later. I nearly had to do a double-take. I wasn't expecting a false alarm. Looking back, I don't remember any other false alarms. If anything, Granny could be described as hospital-resistant; she was always willing to wrap a knee or even stitch up a stab wound before she would let you go to the hospital. We had a ghetto pharmacy in the closet that rivaled most drug stores. There was a collection of every medication and prescription known to man: antibiotics, pain killers, blood pressure pills. You name it; she had it. Oddly enough, that habit of hoarding prescriptions was carried over to my Mom and ultimately myself. While its origins are likely found in the lack of easy medical care in rural Kentucky, I do it out of habit, a habit I picked up because of nurse Granny.

As it turns out, that trip to the hospital technically wasn't a false alarm; it just wasn't heart-related. Granny had gallstones and received medication or treatment at the hospital that night, and she was sent on her way. When Granny got home, her mood was noticeably better. While I suspect she still had some pain, I imagine the weight of the world had been lifted from her shoulders as she now knew it wasn't more severe. In the days following the hospital trip, the mood around the house was light, and the only memorable events were heated discussions about whether to get gallbladder surgery. Granny's concern was that if she got the surgery, she wouldn't be able to partake in the rich, fried, southern foods she loved. Her initial plan was to leave it in place and just manage the symptoms if they reoccurred. This approach seems a little ridiculous; as a person with a significant cardiac history, she was willing to leave an angry and inflamed gallbladder in place so that she could still partake in foods that specifically caused further damage to her heart. While there is something to be said about death's inevitability and the "well, you've got to die of something" attitude, even I thought this position was a little dumb at thirteen years old. In the end, the doctors won out. The argument that ultimately persuaded her was that as long as the gallbladder was intact, they could remove it using an endoscope, leaving only a few tiny holes and requiring a night or two in the hospital. That approach was compared to the option of leaving it to become more inflamed or rupturing later, which would lead to the need for a much more invasive operation. Surgery was scheduled for the following week, and life moved on.

It was almost Christmas break, and I had started spending a lot of time with my new best friend and neighbor, Scott. Scott and I were the same age, played footballs, liked RC cars, liked bikes, rode ATVs, and most importantly, liked girls. We were quickly inseparable in our quest for girls, and where do you go at thirteen to find girls? The skating rink. Our local rink was brand new and more than twice the size of any others in the area. It featured colossal concession and game areas along with a sizable socializing area. The social space was maybe forty-by-twenty feet and featured large plywood boxes covered in carpet serving as benches bordered by lockers on two sides. A short concrete wall surrounded the hardwood rink, and a DJ booth was elevated in the corner. After 8:00, they turned down the lights and turned up the music. There might have been 200 to 300 teenagers on a Friday night, and at least half of them were girls. Scott and I were in heaven. Scott seemed to have a little more experience with girls than I had. I chalk up this enhanced skill set to him having older brothers and sisters to serve as examples. Either way, we tried to figure the whole girls thing out, little by little. At that time, I was a good-looking kid but not particularly adept at talking with girls, and my success ratio of getting a phone number or date would have maybe been thirty to forty percent compared to Scott's seventy-five plus percent. One strategy was Scott, and I served as wingmen to each other and often came as a package deal to any pair of interested girls. Often, he would like a girl, and the girl would like him, but they couldn't do anything unless he found someone to hang out with her friend—Justin, to the rescue. I was happy to play second fiddle as it was good practice, and let's be honest, at that age, managing to hold a hand or get a kiss at the end of the night was about all that was at stake. By the time winter was in full swing, it was official; I had a new hobby, and it was girls.

The day of Granny's surgery came and went, and initially, everything had gone well. So well, I can't even remember the specific day or even days afterward. The day she was supposed to get discharged came, and there was a problem. Papaw told me it wasn't anything significant, but there was an infection, and they would need to keep her for a few more days for it to go away. I would go with him after school and evenings to visit her a couple of times a week. My first memory of anything being off was when we saw her, and she was pretty sleepy. Up until that point, she had always been up and awake, ready to pull out the tubes so she could walk home. Granny would get better over the next few weeks, have a minor setback, and get better again. While her recovery took a long time, there weren't any indications she wouldn't eventually get better. It was slow progress, but Granny was a little better each day. It is possible that in my girl-induced haze, I missed a clue or conversation that more clearly explained what was taking so long. Still, to my best recollection, it was just a slow recovery from an infection inside the abdomen by a woman with a significant health history and age.

Granny's recovery dragged into weeks and even months. Papaw was the kind of spouse that didn't just visit the partner at the hospital; he was a camper. He would simply show up in the morning and spend the entire day into the evening. Eventually, he would come home at the end of visiting hours, and he would do it again the next day until she came home. It wasn't uncommon during that process to not see him the entire day, only in the morning and again at night when he would give you the day's progress report and update. Over time, I ended up visiting a little less–maybe around two or three times a week—and I was usually parlaying the trip to the hospital into a ride to the movies or the skating rink so Scott and I could chase girls. Looking back at that time in my life, I am faced with a few observations and truths that are uncomfortable and expected. The thirteen-year-old me was eventually trading away time with my de-facto parent for time with girls. As a parent of teenagers, I know that it is entirely normal. As I watch my daughter and sons mature, they very clearly traded time with Mom and Dad for times with friends and the other sex. What I was missing at the time that I now see was that Papaw saw this also. He was always trying to be understanding and tolerant, but he was also very aware of the need not to let me take my absence too far. Papaw never let me go a week without seeing her, and I am grateful. I don't think he did that because he thought she wouldn't be around. I think he did that because he saw my movement away from her—no matter how natural—as what would eventually be a movement away from him. Papaw was afraid of his perfect baby boy growing up and losing his best friend.

By the summer between seventh and eighth grade, my practice with the girls had paid off. I had graduated from landholding, got my bachelors in kissing, and was thinking of enrolling in the college of heavy petting. Scott and I were still regulars at the skating rink on the weekends and managed to both have successful years in school. Just after July 4th of that year, Scott and I went to the skating rink, and it happened. The student became the master, and I achieved what was greatness in my thirteen-year-old mind. I scored a date with Sara, and Scott had to come to keep her friend, Jenny, company; things had come full circle, and I was in my element. Sara was almost two years older than I was and a lifeguard at the local YMCA. Thin and tan, she was the most attractive girl I had gotten a date from until that point. Her dark, curly hair and green eyes punctuated her freckles and sweet demeanor. On top of getting a date, I had even gotten a small peck of a kiss at the night's end. We made arrangements to meet at the YMCA pool Monday, which was her day off.

Upon being picked up after skating that night, I was given even better news: Granny was coming home on Monday after more than six months of recovery. Papaw said he would need my help getting the house cleaned up and ready for her return. He had also mentioned that he wanted to take me to look at the new car that he wanted to get for her. It was good news all around. Papaw also graciously agreed to give Scott and me a ride to the pool on Monday morning and planned to pick us up in the new car that evening after he got Granny home that Monday. July 11th, 1994, looked like it would be a perfect day.

Monday morning came, and I was nervous. Today was the day I was hanging out at the pool with Sara and Jenny. I was worried because she didn't know how old I was. She had her license and a job, and I had just graduated from toys cars. I had always been able to adjust my maturity and effective age upward out of necessity. Whether that necessity was sneaking into visiting hours or dating Sara, I was good to go. A plan was hatched with Scott and I am having Papaw drop us off at the edge of the parking lot so that we would walk up and they wouldn't see us getting dropped off by our parents. Feeling considerably slicker than we were, we executed the plan and, by 11 a.m., found ourselves sitting at the pool. Sara was hotter than I remembered and smiling as she came running up to me wearing a bikini and sunglasses. The first thing she did was give me a giant hug, almost hanging her whole weight onto me. I was nearly speechless and almost wondered if I was on candid camera or was being pranked. She then asked me to put sunscreen on her back—which I did as she held her hair up in a tight bun so I could get her shoulders. After a few hours of hanging out, we all grabbed some food. Scott had already talked poor Jenny into what certainly wasn't either of their first French kisses by that time. Sara looked at me, and while I didn't get the complete treatment

Scott did, I got one of that mouth half-open, slow, and deliberate ones you see on TV. We made our way back to the back corner of the pool. We sat down in the sun—Scott by my side and Sara leaning back on me. At that moment, in my thirteen years of life, I was just about as close to being the king of the world as I could imagine. Looking over Sara's shoulder towards the front gate, something caught my eye. It was Papaw, looking a little frazzled. My heart sank; he had ruined it. He came to get us in the new car, but he was early. I still hadn't told Sara how old I was. But why was he here, I asked myself. We weren't supposed to get picked up until we called sometime around six. Just then, I saw my mother rushing down the hill after him. What now? They had been fighting a lot lately, and she drank more. Why did she have to show up here, causing trouble and embarrassing me? My Mom had done him before; she would get drunk, roll up on me, start yelling and hitting, no warning, no rational reason, just a drive-by beating. While I was fishing at a lake, a minor league game, football practice—all of those had been scenes of those drive-by beatings. I guess it was a good thing Papaw was there to try to stop her. It was embarrassing, but at least I could just say she was crazy…

I walked over to them, and Scott followed pretty closely. Something was off; they both were distraught, but not at each other. My mind raced to figure out what was going on. Wasn't he supposed to be picking up granny from the hospital around one? If something were wrong with Granny, he wouldn't have left her there. Maybe something was wrong with Rick, my Mom's boyfriend. Had he gotten hurt? As I got closer to Papaw, I could see him crying—not like a reserved cry you instantly swallowed back down, but a full-on ugly sorority girl cry. Just as he started to say the words to me, it made sense. It wasn't that I was hearing what he was saying; I had solved the puzzle just as he was telling me. Papaw would have never left Granny, and he would have just sent my Mom if she was dying—SHE WAS ALREADY DEAD.

Gloria Dean Hodge ~December 13th, 1934- July 11th, 1994,

I instantly started to cry and hugged both of them. In that moment of ultimate sorrow and sadness, we shared an embrace that may have never been equaled between the three of us again. My Mom ushered Scott to get our stuff. In moments we were off. Sara and Jenny—while shocked by the events—certainly understood. The hospital was only a mile or two from the YMCA. We pulled up to the side of the emergency department, and I could see Rick and my Uncle Donny. My Aunt was there, ready to receive my Mom's embrace. Somehow everything still seemed like it was happening in a rush like we were in the midst of an emergency. People always talk about the perception of time adjusting to traumatic events, and it wasn't that. That was legitimately everybody rushing around in chaos. I just assumed they were maybe still trying to perform CPR or shocking her, something like that. When I walked into the room where she was, I saw her lying on a bed. She had a sheet pulled up to her underarms, and each arm was neatly at her sides. Her eyes were closed, and her skin was pale, almost yellowish. Her arm was bruised and stained where the IV was inserted. I took a few steps forward and placed my hand on her left forearm halfway up. The texture was dry, and the skin was a little swollen and cold, shockingly cold. Maybe it was good. It was hard because that sensation of touching cold flesh can set in the reality of death, no matter how much you don't want it to be true. Would I have plead for the doctors to do more if it had been warm? Would I have tried it on my own? I don't know, but the moment my hand touched her, it was real, and I wasn't going ever to have her again.

My Uncle, Donny, came in and found Scott a few minutes later. He took him back home and got him away from this mess. In all of my planning and prepping for the worst circumstance, I knew Donny would have a part to play somewhere, and I was so grateful for that. Unfortunately, that wasn't his last engagement performing the shittiest job in the shittiest of circumstances.

In the end, Granny died of a blood clot while she was riding in the car on the way home from the hospital. Surely something jarred loose from the excitement and bustle of the first day of activity in six months. They had stopped at the car dealer after leaving the hospital to look at the brand-new Cadillac. Light yellow with cream interior, chrome, and even a fake, wire-wheel-styled spare tire on the back. She had loved it, and they left the deposit and were going to come back and get it the next day. After six months in the hospital, she was finally out on a beautiful sunny day. She was talking with Papaw at an intersection and suddenly slumped over. Thinking quickly, he turned on his hazards and drove as fast as possible to the ER a few miles away. He ran stoplights and weaved through traffic. He recalled being scared he would get in a wreck, but somehow, he knew he didn't have time to wait for an ambulance. Granny had been at the hospital for almost two hours by the time I got there.

Granny's funeral was beautiful. A blanket of roses covered the funeral home's most expensive rosewood casket. She wore a black dress and an old-fashioned, white nurse's cap. The folds and bends were perfect, and the thin, black, silky ribbon denoted she was still in charge. Her grave sits just to the left of Billie's in the shade of a dogwood tree. That very same dogwood tree that had helped her select Billie's grave a dozen years before.

The day she died, Granny was only inches away from the love of her life and ultimate protector. She was only a few hours away from seeing her replacement son and hearing the story about how he had an older girlfriend. She was only a day from a new Cadillac. Most importantly, though, she was already in the arms of her real son, Billie, after thirteen years. Thinking about that makes you wonder if any other measure of time or distance matters.

That entire year, I thought, "I had it all figured out," and wondered, "will she ever come back." I never knew for sure, but "life moved on." In the end, I lived my year like any other, with all of the false confidence and bravado only a thirteen-year-old boy could muster because I just knew "July 11th, 1994 was indeed looking like it was going to be a perfect day".

That day I learned nothing was guaranteed.

Chapter 6

Science Teachers, Graham Crackers, Mullets, and Oakley's©

The remainder of the summer of '94 went quickly. Following Granny's death, things for me had generally fallen back into a routine. The only defining distinction was that I saw Papaw more. As he no longer had daily trips to the hospital to take, he began searching like so many widowers do. He was seemingly searching for something else to complete his days, define his identity, or fill the now empty time. His first adjustment was to put the full six acres of grass on a twice-weekly cutting schedule. Papaw was also apt to drop in on his friends and acquaintances. I always found it odd to stop by someone's house without first giving a call or having specific plans. Not for Papaw—he would just show up. I'm sure he was also uncomfortable with these visits, but his extreme sense of being lost and lonely without the love of his life surpassed that lack of comfort. As that summer ended, life for Papaw and I had established a new normal. I was aware of how lonely he was becoming, but as a teenager, there wasn't much I could—or more accurately—was willing to do. The pull of friends, girls, and hobbies was too strong. While I theoretically could have spent more direct time with him, that was only part of the puzzle. The other part was that he had lost his best friend and companion, and a thirteen-year-old boy would never be able to fill that void.

By the fall, the school was starting, and I was going into the seventh grade. Football season was kicking off, and I started hanging around the YMCA quite a bit. I know what you're thinking—it wasn't because of Sara. Though we were still friends, we hadn't continued to date. However, Sara had introduced me to the Leaders Club at the Y. The club is best described as an educational and practical group that helps develop leaders through formal and informal mentoring and teaching. Membership is generally comprised of high-achieving—and in some cases—exceptional teens. The group would take on projects around the Y, from hosting sleepovers and managing sports leagues to providing wait staff at the annual YMCA board meetings. The culmination of one's participation in the club came each year with a week long trip to a school nestled in the Blue Ridge Mountains. That school was, in fact, an entire campus with dorms, classrooms, sports facilities, and a central lodge. The purpose of the week long school was to learn techniques and skills that were useful in "Y" life, but more importantly, in real life.

There would be clubs from all over the south at the school, so space was limited, and there was fierce competition for acceptance. To earn a spot at the school, you had to maintain your active status in the local club the entire prior year and meet certain other expectations. Key performance indicators were grades, participation in meetings, volunteer hours, and ultimately a recommendation and sign-off by the advisor for the club. The club's membership consisted of the teenage sons and daughters of State senators, County Commissioners, lawyers, and doctors. It would be an understatement to say I had bitten off a little more than I could chew. The members were of excellent character and great humans with nearly zero exceptions. While their jobs today vary from CIA agents, professors, YMCA directors, and more, they all have one thing in common: they couldn't have become who they are today without the help of one man. Ryan "Graham Cracker" Graham was about twenty-three or twenty-four years old and had recently graduated from Morehead State College. Ryan was previously a member of the Tri-City leaders club before moving to college and had remained affiliated with the club even while he was away. Ryan was now back full-time and serving as our advisor and program director for the Y. While Ryan's direct influence on anyone inevitably varied, no one he interacted with could say he hadn't impacted them somehow, and I am no exception.

My first memory of Ryan was during one of the weekly leader's club meetings held in a small room barely big enough for everyone to fit into. We had been going over the parliamentary procedure and executing the various formalities of the club business when my beeper had gone off. You heard me right, my beeper or cellular radio pager for anyone born before 1960.

The exact circumstances that led to me having a beeper in the first place are fuzzy to me. It was a time before cell phones and even caller ID. Payphones were the norm, and everyone knew everyone else's phone number. Mine had come from Service Merchandise, a now-defunct precursor to the big box stores and Amazon. The model I had cost $39.95, and you had to pay a monthly fee of three to four dollars for service. It had a neat belt clip and a colorful see-through case. They were becoming popular, and I had always wanted to be popular, so I had to have one. I suppose a beeper was of some utility as I was never home to get phone calls from girls, and I knew better than to rely on Papaw's note taking skills. Over time, my friends and I, who also had pagers, even developed a code system such as "911" and "8008135" to relay important info and ensure a quick call back—you know, real sophisticated stuff.

Following my frantic silencing of the notification, the room was silent for a few seconds, and we resumed the meeting. Confident I had escaped significant consequences, I relaxed. The next activity was the introduction of everyone to the new advisor, Ryan. We each took turns standing up and telling some interesting facts about ourselves. Like a childish version of AA, we stood up and said our name—or more accurately, nickname, where we went to school, what sports we played, and how long we had been in the club.

One particular thing about that club was that most members had been given nicknames. Nearly everyone had a handle that was used almost exclusively in addressing each other. The names were typically derivatives of the real name, such as "Zcourtney," This particular nickname was issued because a lengthy list of all members was put on a large whiteboard one time. Someone left out Chris Courtney, so his name was placed at the end of the list with the added Z to avoid rewriting the complete list. That stuck, and to this day, he is still referred to as Zcourtny, pronounced with a hard Z. Other nicknames had origin stories a little more abstract, but all that mattered was everyone had a nickname, and you couldn't pick your own. That particular circumstance was a problem for me because I knew just how impactful a bad nickname could be and couldn't afford to indulge the Crazy name further. I was also a new member and hadn't had much chance to earn an alternative. Just then, it was my turn to stand up and introduce myself. The second I said I didn't have a nickname, I heard Ryan say, "yes, you do; it's Beeper Joe." From that point forward, I would forever be in that friend group for the rest of my life in that friend group known as Beeper Joe. While it certainly wasn't my first pick, it b was way better than the alternative. It would later get shortened to "Beeper," but it was official.

I stayed involved with Leaders Club for at least the next four years, and the club was incredibly influential in my life. So effective, it's hard to point to any one event as special because they all were. Without the Tri-City YMCA Leaders club, I wouldn't have become the person I am today. When the opportunity arose to charter a new leaders club at our local YMCA, I provided the board with my account of how the club had changed my life. I like to think that testimonials helped push the initiative over the line for its approval. To this day, some of the original members of my leader's school class are still involved in the club, including Sara, who is now the advisor of the Durr YMCA, the replacement for the Tri-City branch that closed in the mid-2000s. Shortly after the new club was chartered, my daughter joined and was able to share some of the same experiences I had growing up. Her advisors were Sara, Danielle, and Elizabeth, all three amazing people and club members from when I had been there. While I like to think Hailey's soul didn't need saving quite like mine, I am beyond proud she also got to attend Blue Ridge Leaders School just like I did. I also can't help but feel a little extra proud that the same people who knew me at her age now get to know her and see just how far things have come.

Much like my experience with the club, my experience with Ryan was also so overwhelmingly good that it's hard to point to any one event in which to highlight. Instead, I have to point to a particular trait Ryan had that, up to that point in my life, I had never truly experienced before. Ryan was an infinitely capable and confident as a young man and always exuded a level of comfort in his decisions or chosen path that was inspiring. That confidence was a willingness to hold you accountable in lockstep with that path and any deviations you took from it. That in itself isn't ultra-unique. Over the years, I have met many people who know exactly what they want and what steps are needed to get there. They have also been willing to demand that you get on board with their vision and are upset when you don't follow the plan dutifully. The difference between Ryan and anyone else I had met up to that point is that Ryan was willing to treat you as an equal, and when you messed up, he was ready to chastise you and, more importantly, explain why your actions were wrong. Ryan would help you see your error and help you empathize with the situation from different perspectives.

Through this process of understanding the error, he would help you chart a path forward from that spot to recover. I fully realize most of you are reading this and confused. You are probably screaming at me through these pages, "hey dummy, that's what a father does," and you're right. Helping a child who makes a mistake understand his mistake and its consequences is precisely what a father does. Helping a child recover from his mistakes and learn from them in hopes of not repeating them is a father's core duty.

While that's something I certainly understand now, in the summer of 1994, that concept was foreign to me as I had never had a Father. I had a caretaker who loved me more than anything in the world, but a true Father, he was not. This is not to diminish what Papaw was to me, as he very much had to work within the bounds of society and patriarchal expectations while I was young. After all, he was only my step-grandfather and a bit of a pushover. It wasn't until around 1994, when it was just us, that he could have possibly started to be a father. However, it was too late; we already had thirteen years of inertia fighting us. Regardless of how it came to be, Ryan Graham was my first "Father Figure" who was willing to teach me how to succeed and fail correctly. He always treated me as an equal; there was nothing off-limits because I was young or inexperienced. If I thought I could do something and had a plan to do it, I was allowed to. Over the next few years, while working at the Y, I built multiple-day camp structures and facilities in the woods, learned how to stripe soccer and baseball fields, became a camp counselor, and coached soccer and hockey teams—despite never having played either sport before. Still, most importantly, I learned how to be a man; I learned all of this from Ryan—and those are just the things I can connect with the first degree. Suppose you extrapolate those lessons he taught me and find examples of them in action across my life. In that case, he is probably responsible or in some way attached to a solid twenty-five percent of anything good I have ever done. While I will never be able to repay him in full for everything he has given me, I made a down payment in the summer of '96. I introduced and facilitated his first dates with his now-wife Jennie. While I'm sure they would have found each other without me, I like to think I made things a little easier—but those are stories for them to tell.

Kevin Beardmore was a young teacher—I am guessing maybe twenty-four or twenty-five. He taught science at the middle school for both the seventh and eighth grades. He was also the academic team coach for the school, and that was how I first met him. I was in sixth grade and tried out for the academic team, but that year had been a little different. There are only two squads in middle school, Varsity, and Junior Varsity, despite three grades in the school, sixth through eighth. That meant there was considerably more competition for a place on the team as you were not only competing for fewer spaces, but you also had to contend with older kids pushing out younger kids—that is a genuine concern when each year of education gives you a leg up on the knowledge needed. You were no longer hoping to be among the eight smartest or fastest in your grade to get a place on the team; you now had to be among the sixteen most talented in the school to secure a spot. Tryouts were over a series of afternoons in his science room after school. There were multiply rounds of questions, a written test, and shuffling of teams. His approach to that process was scientific and exact. He had a rubric or formula for exactly what it would take to do well and what a successful team looked like.

When you weren't competing or testing, you had some downtime, and in Mr. Beardmore's classroom, that was a treat in itself. He was a very hands-on teacher with projects like a full-sized, airtight bio-dome where two students had stayed in the sealed plastic room for several days without leaving to see if oxygen levels could be maintained through plants. He was a pioneer of the Technic Lego sets; we had computer-controlled versions in 1994, many years before they became commonplace. Mr. Beardmore's classroom was also the first time I heard of the Internet. He had a computer that could access AOL and CompuServe. Regardless of how the tryouts worked out, I had gotten a consolation prize by just being invited into his universe.

After a whole week of tryouts, the results were in, and I had made it—but just barely. I was on the JV squad and one of only three sixth graders on the team. We had practices and competitions each week for most of the late fall into the spring. I don't remember much about the wins or losses or our record for the year. I remember the time in his classroom practicing. We had freedom as students that I had never experienced before. We were allowed to have a can of coke or candy bar without getting into trouble. If you needed a hall pass, you just grabbed one off the ledge, no need for some elaborate process or controls. He trusted all kids to do the right thing and gave them the freedom to do just that.

The entire year on the team, I couldn't help but hope and pray he would be my actual teacher the following year when I got into seventh grade. Over the years, I have heard different versions of how the kid's draft operated from the teachers' perspective. In my mind, I imagine a cross between fantasy football and a trading floor on the NYSE. In reality, I'm sure it's different, and it may vary from school to school, but regardless of how it's done, I am convinced to my core that it's not done randomly. Perhaps my draft stock had diminished in other teachers' minds because I had gotten into minor trouble in sixth grade related to living up to that damn nickname. Apparently, breaking a kid's arm across your knee like a piece of firewood is frowned upon, even if he asked you to do it and the principal heard the conversation—Sorry, Curtis. Maybe I did get lucky and won some game of random chance. Perhaps it was divine intervention, or maybe Mr. Beardmore gave up some other prime students to pick me instead. No matter how it happened, it worked out in my favor. I was in Mr. Beardmore's science and math class during my seventh-grade year.

If making the academic team in fourth grade was a turning point for me, being in Mr. Beardmore's seventh-grade class was a launching pad. Mr. Beardmore was progressive in his classroom; he would do things his way with or without the administration's permission. He had combined the periods for math and science into an entire half-day of instruction which was terrific. We got another twenty minutes or more that would typically be wasted in the hallway. That approach also allowed for completing complicated lessons that might not have fit into the exact fifty minutes previously allowed.

Mr. Beardmore was also keenly aware of differing abilities

between students. Since the state of KY forbid the separation of classes based on skill after about 1992, he had a solution. His solution was that our math curriculum would be self-paced in his class. You had to finish the book—each lesson, all the practice problems, and the test for every chapter in the book. After that, you were done. Inevitably that created a situation where two distinct factions of students developed: the doers and the procrastinators. I am sure Mr. Beardmore had known this would happen, and he had a plan. He used the time he wasn't waiting on the kids who did it themselves to give one-on-one instruction to those who needed it. We still had a fixed time each day for math, so he would provide a chapter four lesson for those who needed it and a chapter five-lesson for those who needed that one. That is where phase two of his plan, including student tutors, would also help.

A distinct group of about six students had finished the book by Christmas break. With lots of free time on our hands, we were allowed to do a particular project. It didn't matter what the project was; we just had to submit a detailed, written proposal, including everything from objective, budget, and timeline. He would work with each of us to refine this project until approved. Once we were approved for our special projects, we were given access to a new lab down the hall. The school had been recently remodeled and now included a few classrooms the school didn't yet have the budget for, such as computer labs and our Applied Technology Lab. At that point, the room was an empty science lab being taken over by a group of seventh-graders to do with as we pleased. While everything we did was under the guise of science and our project, I don't remember much about what my project was or learning about science. Instead, we built Lego contraptions and box forts so elaborate that the fire marshal eventually had to get involved.

As you know, all was not well at that point in my life. Granny had gotten sick and was hospitalized, girls were becoming more important than school, and I had some escalating run-ins with principals and authority. I suspect Mr. Beardmore could sense some of this as well; he was always willing to talk with me and ask how things were going, especially after getting in trouble at school. While I don't know if he ever intervened on my behalf in disciplinary actions, he would always have a conversation with me afterward. While he wasn't a Father figure like Ryan would end up becoming, he was an adult who genuinely understood that things in my life were not well. He probably understood how unwell they were as much as anyone in my life, and that alone was the acknowledgment and support I needed.

Coming back to school during my eighth-grade year, I was shocked and surprised to have Mr. Beardmore as my teacher again. It was just for science, but it was a much-needed familiar face as I was struggling, I might not have known it, but looking back, I must have been wearing the heaviness on my face and in my heart for the entire world to see. Mr. Beardmore was still caring and somehow even knew about my Granny's passing. I suspect he had tried to figure out what was up with me and what had changed. He made sure to tell me he was sorry in the hallway after the first day of class.

While I was in Mr. Beardmore's class, there were some substantial changes that year—no free-range learning and no applied technology lab. While the lab was still unused, I suspect the administration had felt our previous use was not up to their high standards. My intuition tells me that the administration may not have looked favorably on Mr. Beardmore playing loose with the rules the previous year and, as a result, put the cuffs on him despite the benefit given to some of the kids. Regardless of the impetus, it was clear that it was time to get down to business and learn a little. Academically, my eighth-grade year wasn't exceptional. I participated in all of my extracurricular activities—at least as long as possible. Once my second or third school suspension came along, I was taken off some of the teams, like speech and drama.

My eighth-grade football season also had a rocky start. Following Granny's death, I managed to get into a fistfight with one of my Peewee football coaches. I maintain that he was a piece of shit and deserved being beaten down by a 13-year-old if for no other reason than the simple fact he couldn't perceive that he was doing pushing me over the edge. I don't hate him or hold any ill will towards him now, but as a kid, his constant nagging and correcting my techniques despite their successes were more than I could bear. I hadn't realized how much of a role my grief and helplessness in the world contributed to him getting his ass kicked by a thirteen-year-old until many years later when I was able to see others struggle the way I did.

Despite being banned from Pewee football, I caught a lucky break. I was allowed to play for the high school's football team because of my talent and the affiliation between my middle school and the high school. That was perhaps some of the only good news besides being in Mr. Beardmore's class that year. The year ended with a dying whimper. I had managed to get into a fight the last few days of school and was suspended yet again. I didn't have the opportunity to say goodbye to any of my school friends, but more importantly, I didn't get to say goodbye to Mr. Beardmore. The following year, Mr. Beardmore was no longer teaching in the district; he had taken a job out of state that, as far as I could tell, was much more deserving of his talents and abilities. I look back on time I had known him with great fondness and take away two key lessons more than anything else from him:

1. Don't be afraid to break the rules or buck the system for the right reasons. If you know something is better, embrace it and commit to it; don't worry about others' thoughts.

2. Be kind and embrace everyone. No one is better or worse, and everyone has abilities in this world. They may not be the same as yours, but they are valid. Have compassion, but do so in every way. Don't be selective about who you do and don't help.

Since middle school, I have reconnected with Kevin (adults get to use first names) again on a limited basis. I was once asked to give an invocation speech to a group of teachers as they were about to start their school year, and I mentioned him in my presentation. I figured it was only suitable to give him the courtesy of a heads-up. I tracked him down and sent him a copy of my speech. He was immensely grateful for my kind recollections of the time, but he did mention he didn't remember any parts of what he did to be special or unique—and that is precisely why he is so special. What he did for me wasn't special or unique—he treated everyone that way. He believed in everyone and was willing to help and foster them in any way he could. To Kevin, he was doing his job, and that is amazing. He is still involved in education today and has undoubtedly affected hundreds of people's lives over the years—just like mine—and may still be unaware of how special he is.

Kevin and Ryan are both very cool guys in their rights; however, I don't think they have ever been so extraordinary as to pull off a beautiful, flowing, feathered mullet and a pair of mirrored Oakley Blades quite like Darrell. Even if they once possessed that level of cool and confidence, it had undoubtedly been gone for a few years by the time Darrell rocked that very look in 1995. I had initially met Darrell when I was around ten years old; he owned the local RC car racetrack, Darrell's Raceway, in the next town. What made that fact incredibly unique was that he was only seventeen years old and still in high school when he owned it. He was an accomplished racer that had been spending every available evening and weekend racing, practicing, and traveling to races. At the time, he was about as close to a professional-level racer as one could get if such a thing existed. He had created the track first as a practice facility for himself and a few friends. By the time I met him, it had evolved into an entire operation.

It was created by filling an old tractor dealership with about a foot of dirt and building workbenches, counters, and a driver's stand around the perimeter. He would hold weekly races and practice sessions, sometimes drawing participants from three states away. It was a rough and tumble crowd, and emotions were consistently high, with grown men nearly getting into fistfights over toy cars. It was a dirt circus, and Darrell was the ringmaster. He would adjudicate the disputes, run the business, and even get up and drive his car. Initially, Darrell's Raceway depended on Darrell as the source of trophies. Since they couldn't afford to buy trophies to hand out as prizes, he dipped into his personal collection and placed new brass plaques on them. When he ran out of his own, he would enter out-of-town races to win some trophies he could turn around and give out the following week at his track. Linda, Darrell's mom, ran the concession stand and hobby shop portion. His dad, Ray, handled general crowd control when he wasn't working out of town as a logger. Once I started becoming a regular at the track, Linda, Ray, and Darrell became my second family. I have already mentioned a little about Darrell's style, which was just an extension of his personality. He was forever different from his peers—not in a wrong or anti-social way, just uniquely confident in who and what he was to the degree that he was immune from his peer group.

He was just as likely to walk in a room and give a high-pitched rick flair "whaoooooooooo" at full volume as he was to drop in lines of authentic CB chatter into regular conversation, like finishing a sentence with "comeback" as if he had just released the mic while driving a Mack truck full of logs down the highway. His uniform was a pair of jeans and work boots with a white t-shirt. He would comb his hair and throw on an unbuttoned flannel shirt over the previous uniform if he needed to dress up.

As circumstances tend to go, my first few interactions with Darrell were quite different than they would be down the road. When I met him, I was an awkward, chubby ten-year-old who was a little spoiled and generally a pain in the ass. He was a mature seventeen-going-on-thirty with all the swagger and cool in the world. While he was always willing to help me and guide me when it came to making changes to my car or improving my driving technique, Darrell didn't have the patience to deal with the other latchkey neediness I exhibited. I would get dropped off at the track by Granny or Papaw and plan to stay till closing. If my car broke or I got bored, I would generally make myself a nuisance—either pestering the other paying adults or hanging out with his mom Linda. Linda didn't seem to mind it much as she and I connected. She was from deep in Appalachia, just like a Granny, and they shared many traits and mannerisms. It must have been a mountain thing, but she could always sense when I was antsy, and she would ask me if I wanted a hot dog; just like Granny, she knew the way to my heart. Looking back, I suspect the similarities with how our moms or mother figures treated us and responded to our needs as kids later allowed Darrell and I to understand each other better than most. But, at that point in time, a deeper understanding was still a long way off. Darrell has had a role in my life in one way or another ever since that first summer at the raceway. It would be a long and not always pleasant journey, but as you will see, his presence or absence played a role in nearly every significant aspect of the rest of my life.

Looking back on my life, there are many more influential people in it than I can cover here—some for the right reasons, some for the wrong. But I am writing about these three in particular because they represent both who I would eventually need to become as an adult if I were going to make it and the essential skills or tenements of what that adult would look like. I could have picked others who had many of the same traits, but I fear that I would have been lost to the world without that perfect combination in concert with my particular flavor of chaos that defined my life.

Chapter 7

Kidnapping and Blackmail 101

When I look back on my life, I am always amazed at the number of missed clues or hints of future events I either failed to see or sometimes saw but failed to act on. I missed a big clue when I was thirteen, but I don't fault myself. The adult me can see it plain as day for what it was, but the teenage me either hadn't had the sophistication needed to see it or if I had the sophistication, I hadn't wanted to believe it could happen.

Shortly after Granny's funeral, my Mom and I had a conversation outside my house. It had been casual, small talk with her asking how Papaw had been doing. She said, "you can stay with him for a while; it will be good because he's lonely without Granny." That statement came and went, and it wasn't until nearly a year later that any of its significance would come into play, even longer before I understood its proper depth. The timing of that conversation was just before my eighth-grade year started and maybe a week before I would have the previously mentioned fight with the coach.

Over the next nine months, time went on, ticking each day and week into the next. I had some occasional hiccups with school and trouble, but given what I had been through that summer, most people quickly dismissed it. My Mom had gotten married to Rick and was doing okay. She would swing between bouts of anger and sadness over her Mother's death but was getting by. One development was somewhat unexpected: the deterioration of the relationship between Papaw, my Mom, and my Aunt. I wasn't one-hundred percent privy to every detail, but it surrounded money and the perception that they were somehow entitled to something following their mother's death. While at some point, I believe Granny received a lump sum disability payment that money had many years previously been lumped into the funds of the marriage with Papaw. I don't know if they wanted just that money back or if they wanted half of the estate—that was never clear to me. I know lawyers were engaged by at least my Aunt and eventuality rebuffed unceremoniously by Papaw and his legal team. I was also aware this didn't sit well with anyone, with my Mom and Aunt feeling significantly hurt and betrayed and Papaw feeling even more alone and sad.

Understanding what came next also helps to understand the Appalachian and Granny's cultures. Generally, Appalachian families are very matriarchal in their operation. They get this way because, for whatever reason, injury, death, or whiskey takes the men away, the women are often left supporting the entire family. This is further reinforced when you have families that experience multiple instances of this—sisters and cousins all banding together to support a larger family unit in what could best be described as a clan. Examples of this in history would be the Hatfields and McCoys or the Bakers and the Whites. This is precisely what had happened to Granny's family; her husband had run away just like her dad had, and she was left to raise the kids and make her way in the world all on her own, just like her Mom had. While I'm sure her Mother's death had all the normal implications the death of a parent has, hers probably also had the added burden of also needing to assume the role of caretaker for the larger group, including her sister's family.

There is also a more nuanced view of this, and it involves the methods by which the matriarchal leaders create support and control in these family units. Often lacking education or traditional trade skills, these women must adapt and scrape to survive. They learn how to deftly manipulate and adjust circumstances for their gain—not for profit, but rather for survival. They don't rob stores or shoplift; they write bad checks. They don't just write a bad check; they have a string of open accounts, bad deposits, and bad checks crossing three counties. When caught, they say they had no choice, they were just supporting their family, and they aren't lying. Everything would have been fine if their ex-husband had just deposited that last check instead of drinking it away. Never mind the fact they knew there was no check coming when the whole thing started. Beyond outward transgressions, they are almost always guilty of inward affronts to the community.

They are not above creating a rumor about a man they know isn't true to keep a daughter from dating him. They are happy to make a phone call in the middle of the night to the wife of a man hard at work on the night shift to sow seeds of doubt regarding his fidelity to that wife. They do this not because of its immediate utility but rather to prime the pumps for future needs. Maybe they wanted the man to quit the higher-paying night shift position to alleviate the wife's false concerns, which they themselves created. This subversion has the effect of freeing up a higher-paying job for their kin to come in and take for themselves. It is very much teenage-girl, high school politics played on the stage of life by the grandmasters of the trade. Another exciting thing about this matriarchal cabal is their willingness to use the legal system and police in their favor. While this seems counterintuitive at first, it protects their inner slights of the law from view by focusing the attention outward. While they are the first to refuse a sheriff's request to search premises or locate a husband with a warrant, they are the first to call the same sheriff with a tip about the woman at church who took her parking spot and may also be selling her prescription drugs. You have to wonder, was the call about the medications, or was it really about the parking spot? Based on what I am about to chronicle for you, it is the parking spot.

I was fourteen years old, hanging out around the house without a care in the world, and I heard a car in the driveway. The driveway was a quarter-mile-long and gravel, so you could usually hear someone with at least a little warning before they got to the house. This had always been useful in the past, such as when I would have giant parties; I could usually turn down the music and hide the beer before the cops could make it to the door. More than I'd like to admit, that very series of events played out many times that summer, one in particular ending in a melee that left me battered and bruised and the house with a distinct rush week vibe. Looking out the window, I quickly identified the unexpected visitor as a sheriff; they had switched from the silver cars with blue lights from my childhood to white cars with blue and red lights, the words sheriff emblazoned on the side. The sheriff came to the door, and both Papaw and I met him. That wasn't my first interaction with Boone County's finest, and to that point, I generally followed the Eddie Haskell approach by being overly polite and mature beyond my years. While I suspect they saw through this right away, I tried never to give them a reason to escalate things—distract and divert, yes, outwardly resist, no.

The sheriff did all the talking. He identified himself and told Papaw and I he was there to take me back to my Mother. At that moment, time slowed, and switches began to flip. The sheriff was rather quickly rebuked with a "the hell you are"—not from me. I was still in shocked silence; It had come from the gentle giant himself, Papaw. I suspect the change in nature caught the cop nearly as off guard as I did. Deftly, instead of escalating the situation, the cop took a step back and tried to explain the context. What came next was several minutes of back and forth between the two covering everything from the money, drinking, drugs, a lack of court order, and accusations that the cop would be complicit in abuse if he helped. They were at a stalemate. The stalemate miraculously ended with the Sheriff leaving and saying that if he came back with the court order, he would have to take me, and Papaw would be charged with custodial interference.

The following day came and went—nothing, no sheriff. Papaw had talked to his lawyers and had been told there wasn't much that could be preemptively done as he legally had no actual relationship with me—he was just my step-grandfather before Granny had died. Hence, he was legally nothing to me. They said that given my Mom's history of drug abuse, drinking, and legal trouble, he could likely win a factual custody dispute, but given my age and the fact she wouldn't receive child support, she probably was just trying to stir things up and didn't actually want custody of me. Their opinion was that this was just an escalation of the fight around money and possible inheritance and that nothing would come of it. While the lawyers technically might have been right, they erred in two ways:

1. They underestimated the complexity of the situation.
2. They must not have ever met a woman from Appalachia who felt she had wrongly or rightly been scorned.

Day three of the standoff started around 10 a.m.; the sheriff was back—correction, the sheriff's department was back. Having been surprised by the resolve displayed by Papaw in the first encounter and perhaps being tipped off to the intent to resist, they came in four cars deep. Instead of asking and debating, they carried a court order to take me. The entire process took maybe three minutes to get me into the car. I didn't fight, but I certainly didn't make their job easy. I was happy to tell them how big of dirt bags they were and how small their dicks must have been. I still have hostility to the department and the specific officers to this day. While I know they were doing their jobs, it is evident to anyone with half a brain what was going on and that actual abuse was happening to me through the manipulation of their department and the courts. Some of those sheriffs were my football coaches and friends of Papaw. They knew us and our circumstances yet didn't have the balls to call for cooler heads before putting a fourteen-year-old in cuffs and forcefully taking him from the only home he had ever known.

I noticed one thing during all of the commotions: I saw a face I hadn't seen for some time.

I was first taken to a station and then by cop car to my Mom's house in old Burlington—you know, the house Papaw had rehabbed for her and sold to her for $10,000. She was there waiting in the driveway with her husband, Rick. I then saw a familiar face again, the same one who had been at Papaw's less than an hour before. My mind raced, and I couldn't figure out why or how my current presence in the back of a cop car and him showing up for the first time in years were connected. I didn't understand what I was seeing—he was warmly talking to my mom. What the fuck was my Dad doing there? Once the sheriff got to the driveway, he offered me some advice, and that was to calm down. He told me if I fought with him, he would have to arrest me, and I would go to juvenile detention, probably hurting Papaw's chances of getting me back. I am not sure why he offered that particular advice, or how he managed to do it in a way that allowed me to resist every urge and instinct I had to fight, but it connected. I tried to calm down and agreed not to fight. Deep down, I thought I could always fight once he was gone. He let me out of the car and took the handcuffs off.

The cop pulled away, and I just stared at them—all three assholes in their own way. I said something to Rick. "How could you let this happen? Papaws is a better place for me; she is just doing this for money." The look on his face said everything; his head dropped, and he went inside the house. My Mom quickly retorted that I was out of control and getting into trouble, that the house was a party house with who knows what was going on. My Dad started attacking how I dressed, saying it was like a punk gang member, which perplexed me. I had on a polo shirt, a pair of khaki shorts, white tennis shoes with no socks, and a white Morehead State College (my role model's alma matter) hat perfectly formed to my forehead. Preppy college kid, maybe, frat boy sheik sure, pretty much anything but what my Dad had suggested. I asked him what he was doing there, and he said you're coming with me. The absurdity hit me and felt surreal.

Nothing made any sense. My Mom wanted me the day before; I assumed she was the one that got the court order. What did my Dad have to do with any of this?

He had me get in his car without answers or explanation, and we drove. I didn't say a single word to him for the entirety of the three-hour drive nor the next several days following. I was now going to be living with him and his girlfriend in a small, single-wide trailer. I didn't know where I was as there were so many twists and turns that I couldn't keep up with. I knew it was in the mountains, and there wasn't much of anything around. Despite the circumstances that had gotten me to that place, it was OK. The girlfriend was friendly and pleasant; she always offered me food in typical Appalachian style. She was thin and wore her years heavy; her skin was tan and rough, punctuated by several tattoos that hadn't been legible since the '70s. The description of the motorcycle gang Barbie best personified her. I'm not using her name because she was innocent and just along for the ride in the scheme of things. My Dad was firm in his resolution and was decidedly punitive in his approach. He didn't want to discuss me going back with Papaw and said stuff was going to change, that I needed to learn respect and responsibility—you know, all of the real properties fathers who are present and care want their kids to learn. It was almost as if he had found a book or manual on doing what he was attempting to do to me; it was so foreign and alien to him. Responsibility had never been his strong suit, and I suppose I was impressed with his conviction in a weird way. He would say the words with such confidence and force, but seconds later, like a lost child, he didn't know what came next; insecurity with his new role crept back in. Maybe it wasn't that he was uncomfortable in that role as he does have another son; perhaps he was uncomfortable with how he happened to find himself in that role with me.

Based on my life until that point, I immediately got to work remedying my situation. Please make no mistake about it; I am at the absolute core of my being a wild animal. I am able and willing to fight when faced with overwhelming odds. Whether it's at the end of a gun, under the bottom of a football pile, or in the woods of Eastern Kentucky, I will survive and win. Sensing his trepidation or weakness, I saw an opportunity and went to work. I took the lessons of Granny and my Mom to lull him into a sense of comfort. I openly accepted my new surroundings. I dropped little hints to his girlfriend that this wasn't so bad. I embraced household chores and would even ask for stuff to do around the yard to pass the time. The first week had gone by quickly, but I missed Papaw and worried about him. I didn't know if he got arrested that day when they took me. It would be another week until I had any answers. After a little while, I had a conversation with my dad that went like this, "hey, regardless of whether or not I ever live back with Papaw, I have friends there, and they deserve to know that I'm OK."

While that first round wasn't successful, I didn't expect it to be easy, and I regrouped to try again. I was generally never alone in the house—my Dad would be there most of the time, but it would occasionally be just his girlfriend and I for a few hours a day. After a little while, she started leaving me alone for maybe thirty minutes at a time while she went to the store to get cigarettes. I could act in these brief opportunities, but I had to have a plan. I needed to get away from that place, but something in my mind also told me I needed to have a way never to have to come back to that place. If I just ran away, I would be screwed. I didn't have money, a ride, or even a fundamental understanding of where I was. How was I going even to get back home? If somehow I did get back home, what would just keep the cops from coming back and re-taking me and maybe putting Papaw in jail?

Over the next week, I started planning. The first thing I did was figure out where I was, which was easy enough. I found some mail with an address—Inez, KY, a full 3:45 from where I came from. The second task was to figure out a way home and contact the outside world. Remember the pagers I talked about? They were going to come into play again, but it was risky. I only knew a few numbers by heart. I decided to call my most reliable friend's pager and put 911 before and after the number, hoping he would call back immediately. I had gotten the number for the phone I was using from that little piece of paper above the keypad. That was a risk because she would usually only stay gone for thirty minutes or less if the girlfriend was gone. I did not plan to call Papaw because, in my mind, I thought he was in jail. At just fourteen, I had not gotten past the concept of the cop stating flatly that if he came back, Papaw was going to be arrested and how that might not have been true—or even if he were, he would soon be released. The third part of the plan was to make sure I never had to come back.

At fourteen, I was savvy beyond my years and a little devious. I had noticed in one of the rooms of the trailer shoe boxes full of food stamps—good, old-fashioned government monopoly money, food coupons, to be precise. I'm not talking about a couple of books; I am talking about maybe ten shoe boxes full of neatly filed books and envelopes. I knew what they were from my time living with my mom but hadn't seen a booklet in years up until that point. I didn't know what it took to get food stamps, but I was sure the amount of them present in the boxes was way too much for someone to have legally. I had also found a disposable camera in the back of a drawer and a stash of weed under the couch in my rummaging. The elements of the plan were coming together.

1. Page Scott and let him know where I was so someone could get me.
2. Take photos of the drugs and food stamps and evidence of anything else I could find to prove the cops shouldn't send me back if I got caught.
3. Get ready to run with a stash of food and clothes.

After another day, I was ready. I had the address of the trail-er—check. The stolen disposable camera of unknown vintage full of blurry food stamps and pot pictures—check—a call to Scott's pager with 911 before and after—check. The second

Biker Barbie left the house, I sprang into action. The phone was an older wall mount unit. It had started as avocado green, but years of cigarette smoke gave it a nicotine-yellow tinge that highlighted its favorite numbers. The phone's number was written in block numbers using blue ink, crisp and clear behind a little plastic cover, as was the custom back then.

I dialed the numbers, careful to enter the total number into the keypad: 9-1-1-6-0-6-5-5-5-7-4-3-5-9-1-1. The string of sixteen numbers, careful and deliberate, was entered, and I hung up to wait. The anticipation was killing me; my escape relied on Scott's willingness to quickly return a page from a random number he had never seen before. First one minute, then two, then suddenly a ring. It was only the first half of a ring. I snatched that phone up with lightning speed lest someone accidentally hear it from outside. It was Scott asking if someone paged him. I immediately let out everything I knew—the address, the pictures; everything came out in seconds as a giant jumble of word soup. It was so fast that no one could have understood what I was saying. "Dude, calm down, start again," he said. I started again, this time deliberately making sure he had everything. I had asked him about Papaw, and it turned out everything was fine—he didn't go to jail or anything. No one knew where I was, and they were waiting on court dates. Scott didn't have all the details, but it was something—it was hope. I told him my plan. The only thing was that he didn't have a license and didn't know where Inez was. To my shock, he yelled, "Hey Darrell, where is Inez?" Darrell and I had become reunited over the last year, with my age gap seemingly much more minor and our interest in RC cars, real cars, and all things on four wheels filling the void, reuniting us as friends. Darrell replied, "About 4 hours away near West Virginia in the mountains. My Dad logged there, why?"

Scott explained he was talking to me, and without hesitation, Darrell said, "We will be there in three-and-a-half." I immediately grabbed my makeshift go bag and took off into the woods in the general direction of a store I knew was about half a mile down the road. With nothing more than faith, Darrell was driving in my order and that somehow the evidence I had in that old camera was going to fix everything; I ran. I didn't leave a note, nothing, just crept out of that house and went straight into the woods to hide. The terrain was steep, and I had heard there were rattlesnakes, but I didn't care—neither was going to stop me. I planned to hide in the woods behind the store, the agreed-upon meeting point, and wait until I saw Darrell's truck. It was about four o'clock when I talked to Scott and figured Darrell would get there just before dark. You would be surprised how many white 1992 Isuzu pickup trucks existed near Inez, KY. After maybe three false alarms in as many hours, I saw him pull up. He calmly went inside and got a Gatorade, as was his custom, before walking back out and standing next to his truck. He leaned on that truck with the confidence only Darrell could have while committing what could have been any number of felonies coming down there to get me. He didn't care. He knew I was in trouble and needed his help, so he came—end of the story.

The trip back was long. He filled me in on all the details and happenings during my absence. Papaw was aware he was coming down to get me but hadn't had any part of the planning in case things went sideways. As it turned out, Darrell had some hesitation about coming but decided to come anyway. He figured if it was important enough for me to have called like that, it was good enough for him. On the way home, we stopped at a store and got the photos developed, figuring it was best to get the evidence in hand in case something happened. The rest of the right was uneventful, and we made it back to the house around one in the morning. At first, I was hesitant to stay there if the cops came back, but I missed Papaw and wanted to see him, so I had Darrell drop me off at the top of the driveway, and I snuck back to the house in case anyone was watching. It was an emotional reunion, to say the least, with Papaw and I embracing each other with a force that could crack ribs. We both cried and enjoyed our moment of being whole again.

The following day around eleven A.M., my Dad showed back up at the house. Somehow, I was scared and confident all at the same time. Papaw had filled me in on a little of the backstory, and needless to say, it was fucked, even for my family. Unsure how my Dad would react, I let him go first and was relieved to see his tone was conciliatory, and he was admitting the situation was wrong. He confessed he just believed what my Mom had told him and went along with her plan. He didn't know about the pictures I took or the thick handful or envelopes I stuffed into my go bag along with the canned beans and crackers, but no can opener. There was some mention on Papaw's part of "taking care" of my Dad, but in a stunning display of honor, my Dad refused. In perhaps his only good action in the whole ordeal, he rejected what would have likely been $5,000-$10,000 to join Papaw's side in the fight. Maybe it was wisdom—but more likely experience with all parties involved—that led him to decline the offer. I don't know, but regardless of the reason, he had been defeated and, for a second time, wanted nothing to do with the chaos that was this life.

As it was my Dad's inclusion that gave credibility to the custody paperwork originally, once he gave up the fight and we shared my evidence with the attorneys, the matter was quickly closed. The wounds of those three weeks in June of '95 changed me forever. It changed the way I viewed my Mom and Dad forever. It tainted my view on the legal system and law enforcement and ultimately served as another reminder that no one would look out for me but me and maybe Darrell that I always needed to be vigilant.

To give you more of an overall understanding of how these events played out, I will provide, as I have previously, my best adult understanding of events and circumstances. This should be pretty accurate but may lose some details due to how long ago it was and my age when it happened. The entire thing originated with perhaps good intentions combined with greed and guilt on my Mom's part. She had been doing well in her personal life, mainly getting her addiction under control and generally finding a peace she hadn't often experienced. While her mother's death was a setback, it was also an opportunity. This was her chance to prove she could be responsible and was up to the task of keeping the family together. As her Mom and Grandmother did, she would hold it together. Combine this success on her part with her observing from the outside the deterioration and decline that was my life. I had started to get in trouble at school. I was getting in fights often and even had a run-in with the law involving a fight with the coach. While I was hanging on, I was barely doing so, and she felt some desire to intervene.

Combine this genuine desire to step up with a dispute involving money between her and Papaw, and the stage was set. Add on top of this the fact that one of the friends Papaw had been dropping in on was a woman my Mom knew. While the relationship was strictly platonic, that didn't matter to my Mom, it had only been a year, and that was the ultimate betrayal. All of that combined was motivation enough for her to put her plan into action. My Dad was only involved as a pawn. Years earlier, she had somehow managed to get his name retroactively added to my birth certificate in a scheme to get child support from him. That is absurd because she never supported me at any point, so why should she have gotten reimbursed? She had convinced him to go along with this plan to steal me away by promising that his child support obligation would be eliminated once he had full custody of me. That, of course, wasn't true, but he's not a lawyer either. Ultimately, my Mother had schemed and manipulated the plan into action. Once in motion, she realized she wouldn't be able to control me, nor would she want me around, given my displeasure with the situation. I was a rattlesnake—now that you've caught it, what are you doing with it? Her solution was to send me with my Dad many counties away and not tell anyone where I was. The secrecy of my location was used as leverage as she negotiated for custody she didn't want and the money she did want. She got neither money nor custody and lost a son in the end. I doubt that was the outcome she had wished for, but she underestimated just how much of her was in me and how long I could hold a grudge.

That summer, I got my graduate degree in manipulation and even had some classes on blackmail and evidence. The following weekend there was a party at my house. We grilled mountains of steaks, boiled crab legs, and had pounds of potato salad. It was my treat—care of the only victory I had that year: a handful of food stamps I grabbed on my way out the door.

Chapter 8

Amish Sawmills, Paintball and the Birth of an Entrepreneur

Following the great raccoon scandal of sophomore year, I found myself dis-invited from participating in formal education. All avenues were closed to me; I was unwelcome to pay tuition to the diocese of Covington. Since I had fled justice in the previous year's Boone County School debacle, I had never officially been expelled, leaving me to still deal with/serve out the term of that expulsion, which was one year. Ohio was no longer an option as the parking pass situation would necessitate moving, which was off the table. While I was out of legal education options going forward, I had benefited from what was perhaps one of the only lasting gifts given to me by my Mother—the GED she arranged for me. That flimsy slip of paper was all I needed, all I needed to keep the truancy officers away, and all I needed to move forward in my life, ostensibly as an adult. I say move forward as an adult somewhat facetiously but also truthfully.

The summer before my sophomore year, I had been kidnapped and held against my will as a pawn in an ill-fated attempt to extort payment in a probate matter. To get out of that situation, I had turned not to responsible and loving parents or the legal system but rather to my own blackmail and sedition and a lucky phone call to my friends, and somehow it had worked. How could society expect me to have experienced that and go back to a regular school environment and fit back in with kids, talking about riding their bikes or how hard the next algebra test would be? If my distant past hadn't set me up to fail in a school environment, my more recent experiences guaranteed it. To sum it up, everyone involved is lucky it stopped at a few fights, stolen parking passes and releasing a possibly rabid raccoon on a school. The end of the summer of 1997 rolled around; I was only sixteen—no job and no purpose in life. It was time to make some decisions and make them fast.

That year, Darrell and I spent a lot of time together, and he had quickly replaced Scott as my best friend. It wasn't that Scott wasn't still a good friend, but as he still attended high school, roller-skated with girls, and played football, our chances for crossover rapidly declined. Darrell—who was in his early twenties and had a full-time job—was someone I could connect with on a much more practical basis. Darrell offered a solution, sensing I needed something to do after my dis-enrollment from formal education. He and his Father had just bought a sawmill and needed someone to help get it up and running. They needed someone reliable and hard working. Despite my challenges, I was always on time and could never be accused of not working hard. I instantly took the job and hoped to learn the details the next day when I had to meet with his Dad, Ray, who I remembered from the RC car track.

Ray is a formidable man, tall on his own but made even taller by a pair of full-heel logging boots that added another 2.5 inches. He was slim and muscular with a distinctive southern accent. Robert Duvall must have used Ray as a character study for the Days of Thunder movie, for it nearly perfectly captures Ray's delivery and tone. Despite the soft demeanor, you would never think of him as anything other than incredibly intelligent, hard as a rock, and razor-sharp. He was an Air Force veteran, survival school instructor, and a college graduate who had also been logging his entire life. That combination of discipline, intelligence, and the experience was exceedingly rare in a field dominated by backwoods roughnecks and men whose careers are punctuated by significant injuries and the highest on the job death rate in the world. Ray had, at that point, put thirty-plus years into a career that averages only eight.

I met with Ray the following evening to discuss the job a little. He asked me the same questions about experience and skills anyone else would have gotten. It was not a guarantee that I would get this job despite the recommendation by one of the owners. We covered the time of work and eventually got to pay. I was going to be paid fourteen dollars per hour. From my perspective, having only made minimum wage at the YMCA and my other jobs over the previous years, I had hit the jackpot. From Ray's perspective, he was paying me the same rate he would any other man that was willing to trade his time, safety, and back. Ray didn't expect any less of those three from me. There was another catch: we started at 6 a.m. every day, and the sawmill was located about an hour and fifteen minutes south in a town called Ghent. Since I didn't have a truck, I would get a ride each morning with either Ray or his other son, Danny, who would be making the same trip.

Since I didn't drive, I had to stay at the sawmill until they were done each day, even if my work was done, without pay. If I didn't like that arrangement, I could buy my truck and pay for my fuel and leave when I was done. At that time, I had a Mustang I had souped up and modified into a loud, obnoxious beast, but it certainly wasn't suited for the hour-long drive or the rutted dirt roads leading to the mill. By the end of the conversation, I had entered only my second adult-level agreement in my life—the first was with Coach Napier, and now this one was with Ray. After hands were shook, I was off to Walmart to buy a pair of work boots and some gloves. While I didn't know exactly what kind of either to get, I knew what Ray and Darrell's looked like and would see what I could find.

3:45 A.M. came early the next day. I dressed in my most lumberjack outfit—jeans, work boots, a flannel shirt, and a stiff leather belt. I put my gloves in my back pocket and took my first steps in those new boots. Tight and stiff, I franticly tried to break them in before Danny pulled down my long driveway. We were on the road from a quarter till five, and he was listening to country music as I looked out the window at the dark landscape just waking up. Danny was holding a spit cup in the same hand he used to shift his diesel truck; we began to talk. He went through the day's schedule, which meant little to nothing to me at the time. He either did not know it was my first day or, more likely, didn't care. We stopped at a small truck stop about twenty minutes from the mill and grabbed some breakfast in the form of a little, greasy breakfast sandwich. He looked at me and said I had better grab two since we wouldn't be coming back into town for lunch. I was partially shocked because I hadn't even considered lunch. I didn't pack one nor had plans to buy one. I obliged and quickly grabbed a candy bar to go with my bacon, egg, and cheese lunch.

We pulled into the mill right before 6 a.m., which was already full of activity. I noticed a giant mound of sawdust with a long, thin conveyor leading to the apex. The conveyor was slowly dripping dust on the top of the pile at what must have been nearly one hundred feet above the base. I can remember thinking and calculating what kind of volume must be represented in that pile and how many cubic yards of material it contained. Quickly diverted from the mound, my attention focused on the mill itself. The only thing I could think was what a shithole. Its siding was a loose conglomeration of boards and planks that left significant gaps big enough to see inside. Some of those gaps even lined up with ones on the other side, allowing one to see through the building entirely. The roof was rusty metal, come corrugated and some tin standing seam. Sliding doors covered an opening in even rougher shape. I remember one door on the front being half off the track. The stockyard was on two sides of the building; it was covered in stacks of finished wood piled five or six pallets high. Some of the pallets were a nice yellow and appeared freshly cut. Others were a silvery gray, showing evidence of sitting outside for quite some time. We kept driving to the other side of the mill as this first arrival was also my orientation and safety briefing. The back two sides were surrounded by muddy yards the size of several football fields. The mud was black and grainy, like mulch mixed with sawdust and dirt. There were piles of large logs everywhere, sorted and neatly stacked, grouped in categories. At the time, I had no idea what those groupings or categories meant, but I could still clearly tell there was a nuanced and deliberate nature.

In the yard were several semi-trucks being unloaded by a large, rubber-tired loader with forks, and manning this machine was Ray. From that mobile throne, it appeared he could control the entire operation from behind the glass of the cab. While the noise of the equipment made speech difficult, in just that fleeting moment, I was able to see just how effective a combination of exaggerated gestures, eye contact, and the occasional beep of the horn could be in getting the significance of most orders across. I was also able to witness one of the more direct methods he had to communicate, climbing out of the cab. While generally, getting out of the cab was a last resort in my case, it was just to welcome me to the site, tell me to be careful, and that Danny would get me started. Regardless of the message he was giving me, at that moment, a lesson in the significance of stopping the equipment was learned, and it wasn't lost on me, as stopping the machine meant everything else stopped, and that was rarely ever good.

Danny parked the truck, and we went inside. He showed me the office area, a small ten-by-ten block room with a small window and a metal door. Next was the bathroom, an old, wooden outhouse over a hole filled with sawdust. We ended at the sink, kitchen, and water fountain, all served by an old frost-proof well-head. It was the kind with a large D-shaped handle you pulled up to turn on and slammed closed to reduce the stream of water leaking into the mud to a trickle. Before continuing the tour, I will give you a little history of the sawmill to provide context. Darrell and his father had just bought the property earlier that summer. Before their purchase, it was owned by an Amish community and was used to saw rough lumber and siding for use on barns. Those large stacks of unused barn siding and fence rails made up the random silver bundles around the property and were included with the purchase.

As it was an Amish sawmill, it made no use of electricity with only minimal lighting and switches haphazardly strung about the building after the sale. That also explained why the building was left essentially open—for light. Kerosene lanterns and sawdust didn't mix, so the Amish worked with the sun and took advantage of all the natural light. Since the Amish didn't embrace technology, it also meant the mill was made—or, more correctly, assembled—from various parts of antique mills and industrial equipment that had far outlived any usual definition of obsolescence and had moved into existing solely as artifacts in museums. This one mill had been lost to time in Ghent, Kentucky. Resuming the tour, I got my first look at the business end of the mill. The sound was deafening, and it physically hurt to walk to that side of the production floor because of the noise. The noise was coming from everywhere. There were high-pitched squeaks from below, deafening roars to the left, flapping, rhythmic cadence from above, then suddenly, there would be a rattling of what seemed like a roller coaster followed by a deep, cartoonish sawing sound. I will go into a bit of description to get a better understanding of just what this operation was. I am also including a YouTube link showing a video of a nearly identical unit in operation.

Sawmill Description: What it was

The principal saw, or head saw, was about five feet across, made of steel, and featured around fifty hardened carbide teeth. It was mounted directly on a shaft coming from the power source, and the overhead blade was driven with a series of pulleys and belts from the same single power source. A shaft powered nearly every item in the mill. When initially constructed in the 1890s, the mill would have used a single steam engine or possibly an early diesel engine to power the entire mill. While the main blade would have been powered with a direct connection, the various conveyors, trim saws, and dust removal systems would be powered by an infinitely complex series of shafts, pulleys, and gears connected to that main power shaft. In this mill the original steam engine was replaced by part of a semi-truck. The previous Amish owners must have watched Mad Max during Rumspringa because they ditched the steam engine and replaced it with pieces cut directly out of an over-the-road truck. The engine, radiator, transmission, and some of the frame rails were all crudely cut from a full-sized semi-truck and grafted in like a macabre steam-punk Frankenstein's monster. The power was diverted directly out of the regular transmission and connected to the existing main shaft like a truck drive shaft. While I never saw it done, it was theoretically possible to shift gears on the transmission and run the entire operation at a higher speed, like going from first to second in your car. This grafting of a modernish power plant meant that the process still depended on a single diesel engine screaming at 3750 RPM, billowing black smoke under load to run everything. This also dictated no speed controls, throttles, or emergency stops either. If you needed to stop everything in a hurry, you had to apply a brake and wait for the total inertia of every pulley, shaft, blade, and belt to come to a stop.

Safety Concerns: Stuff that would kill you

Based on the setup, there were three significant areas and one minor area of danger that one had to be aware of.

1. Directly in line with the blades, fore or aft of the knife, was a danger zone; anything kicked out by the sword was likely to travel that path. This was also the blade's path if the main shaft broke or the edge cracked.
2. Anything at either end of the carriage. This is the roller-coaster cart the log moves back and forth into the saw blade. Once placed into motion, nothing would stop its activity, not a five-foot saw blade and certainly not a human.
3. Anything in line with the crosscut saw. The problem

with this saw was that it ran directly off the same shaft as everything else. You operated this saw from a position slightly offset, knowing if it caught, there was nothing you could do to stop it, and your only option for safety was to be out of the way.

4. The belts, chains, shafts, and pulleys all represented their own risk, but more than one hundred years of homemade guards and ingenuity had eliminated the most common hazards. That guard hammered out of an old tin can might have looked funny, but it did its job just as well as a current OSHA-approved warning label-covered version.

The Human Element: Where the 400-lb gorilla meets the tool

You should understand the roles now that you're slightly more knowledgeable on nineteenth-century sawmill equipment. The entire process is controlled by the sawyer who runs the levers and makes the decisions on efficiency and strategies. There is also a loader, which was handled in this case by the rubber-tired loader from the yard. The cut-off operator is the next person in the line, and he has one main job and, depending on skill, energy, and brainpower, maybe half of a few others. His primary job is to operate the swinging cut-off saw, first pulling it across to create a straight edge on one end of the board and then pulling it across again once the desired length is reached. Reading a measuring tape is entirely too much responsibility for this role; a saw stop is set up at the end whenever possible. The cutoff man can simply slide the board to this stop and make his second cut, ensuring a perfect length. Once the board has its last crosscut, it proceeds to the end of the line. It's the stacker's job to sort through the finished lumber that just needs the ends trimmed. The stacker's home station involves him taking the boards off the end of the rollers and placing it in a neat, precise stack that corresponds to their size. Every once in a while, if both the stacker and the cutoff man are similarly skilled, they would develop a rotation going through slabs, cutoff, and stacking while using the least amount of movement and steps possible.

As my tour with Danny concluded, he introduced me to the team I would be working with on the sawing crew. Danny was running the pallet-making unit I would also eventually work with, but that was a smaller, less formal affair that only served to punctuate and distract from the majority of my work. I only have first names, and even they are a little fuzzy in memory, but I will do my best. The sawyer, the second in command for the entire mill, was a gruff old man named Clifford with a big belly, about fifty to fifty-five years old. He was somewhat unkempt looking; he had square, wire-rimmed glasses with the gradient tinting that was so popular in the late '70s. Clifford had all the aura of an Elvis impersonator—but only in the standard, playing-Wednesday-night-at-the-Holiday-Inn way. Clifford certainly had some operational intelligence, and he knew enough to calculate the best practices to saw up a given size of wood given the choice of stock before him. He had a reputation of being pretty tough and had a long history in the logging business, mainly in Pikeville and the mountains of eastern KY. His communication skills varied from situation to situation; he might start a day with a sailor's rant about whatever was broken and finish it off by calling me a dumb sum-bitch who's just looking up at the sky while he was needing something from you—he was a real patient fellow.

Clifford stayed in a travel trailer on the property out past the log yard during the week and would go home to parts unknown in eastern Kentucky on the weekends, leaving every Friday as soon as the paychecks were handed out. Johnny was a man in his fifties that could have passed for his seventies. He had been ridden hard and put up wet. Johnny communicated not unlike Sling Blade, with the same gravelly grunting and an almost monosyllabic tone barely audible and nearly always indecipherable. He was missing both the upper and lower front teeth, and I would later learn he subsided entirely on a diet of potted meat product and long-strand chewing tobacco. I never saw him spit, so I must assume he swallowed every bit of that juice as part of his diet. Johnny also lived on the property like Clifford, but he didn't go back every week. I'm not sure what he did on the weekends, as he also didn't have a car. He would only go home every other week at the most and sometimes seemed to stay for a month or more. Johnny's accommodations were another old travel trailer on the property, but this one was much less inviting than Clifford's. I never got within ten feet of it—mainly because of the smell, but it looked decidedly third world in its appearance. Johnny shared that trailer with his son, Clarence, who also worked on the crew.

Clarence was about twenty, but in typical Pikeville fashion he looked like he was at least thirty. He had the facial features and posture that can only come from being beaten by the world. Like his Father, he subsided on a steady diet of potted meat products and crackers. Unlike his father, Clarence was capable of full verbal communication in English and had some points of interest that crossed over with mine. He would occasionally talk about cars and girls from time to time, but we were never more than coworkers at best. A few months after I started, he eventually quit the sawmill. I got the impression he might have gotten a girl pregnant, which, while shocking, could have been possible, and he was wanting to make more money to help support his growing family. Clarence had always talked about leaving the sawmill . By the end of summer he had taken the test for a new job at the Toyota plant. Either a hidden savant or perfectly tailored to fill a certain quota, he ended up getting that job, and I never saw him again.

Concluding my first day, I sat in Danny's truck on the long ride home and thought about what I had just experienced. I don't know if I was more shocked about the sawmill or its cast of characters. It was surreal—everything from the five-foot-tall cartoon-style saw blade spinning at mach Jesus to the flapping leather belts in the ceiling thumped out a rhythm you could work to. Up until that point in my life, I had never met someone from a foreign country, and now I had met three from Pikeville—wherever that was at. I dozed off at some point and woke up just as we pulled into my driveway. As I got out, Danny said, half-kidding, "Have you had enough, or do you want me to pick you up tomorrow?" Not sure how to answer, I said, "Pick me up tomorrow," and walked to the house in awkward silence; not sure what he was thinking, I had made the commitment to Ray and fully intended to work the rest of the year at the sawmill.

Early the following day, Danny picked me up, and we were back on the road. We stopped for food just as before, but I was a little more deliberate in my selections this time. We got to the sawmill, and over the next ten hours, I put in what would be one of the most challenging days of work in my life. We stopped for lunch, and all I could do was lay on a fresh stack of wood. I surveyed the damage; I had already worn out my first pair of soft, comfortable leather gloves, and my feet were blistered from the stiff boots. On top of the blisters, I had managed to smash my toes on my right foot as those boots were only rigid toes, not steel-toed. Luckily it wasn't catastrophic, but as I would find out, it was a mistake more common than you would think. Remembering a section from The Jungle by Upton Sinclair, some things never change. It is still a reality today that inexpensive goods made for people with limited resources have a tendency to look and imitate actual quality products but fall short of the quality products in performance and durability. Danny commented that my boots wouldn't last the week, and indeed they didn't. That weekend, I managed to get some actual quality boots and gloves from a real store to the tune of nearly four hundred dollars in 1997 money for both. That was just gloves and boots. I was told winter gear was even more critical and more expensive.

I showed back up to work with my new boots the following week. They were the same model and style as Ray's; I figured he knew what the best ones were, and he noticed when he saw them, commenting in front of everyone that they were nice and very pricey. I had also started to try a new habit that week of grabbing some extra food such as Lunchables and Little Debbie snacks to put in the fridge. These extras were not intended for me but for the rest of the crew. The week before, I had noticed that every day, for breakfast, lunch, and dinner, the sawmill crew—Clifford, Johnny, and Clarence—would eat a can or two of potted meat product. They had a whole tray or case of the stuff on top of the fridge. They would sometimes have a slice of white bread or a few saltine crackers they spread it on its pasty consistency, a cross between cat food and pate'. They would use their fingers or a flat wooden, spoon-shaped stick to spread it. I always wondered why they would never use their large, folding pocket knives with dark-red handles that each carried. They all had them, and as far as I could tell, they appeared to be a standard issue for any fighting-age male coming out of Pikeville. They would wash down this meal—if you could call it that—with black coffee of unknown origin and age. While I couldn't tell how fresh or hot it was, it was evident that the coffee was ink black and strong, coming out of a green Stanley thermos.

It was around the middle of the second week when I had made the first of many mistakes with that crew. There had been a stray dog hanging around the mill most days—it was a blue healer and somewhat of a character. He would do anything to find a little food, even climb a ladder to get a sandwich if needed. At lunch on perhaps my third or fourth day, I walked over to the fridge, grabbed a small can of potted meat product off the top, and opened it for the dog. Nearly as soon I handed the dog the small tin, Johnny and Clarence both piped up. While I have no idea what Johnny said, Clarence was not happy. He was furious. I had given the dog their food and said it wasn't mine to give; not knowing if he was joking, I just ignored it at first. He then stood up, and I knew what his intentions were in an instant. Resolved to not getting in a fight just yet, I said, "Hey, I'll give you the money for it." Clarence responded, "What would I do with your money? I don't have a car to go get it." Quickly making mistake number two, I told them I had been bringing extra food for them to eat and leaving it in the fridge. My intention with the response had been to appease and placate him;

it instead served only to fuel the fire. Within seconds, I found myself toe-to-toe with a coworker, and I had no idea why. We were broken up before blows were thrown, but I was ready if it went that direction. The rest of the day, I worked with Danny on the pallet crew, somehow feeling indignant and superior at the same time. As we wrapped up for the day, I got into Danny's truck for the long ride home. That ride would be a little different than most, and I remember it today.

Danny started the conversation by asking me what I thought had happened that day at lunch and why they had gotten so mad at me. I went through my childish and arrogant responses—maybe it was because they were rednecks, perhaps they were jealous, etc. He stopped me there. He looked at me with total disappointment and said, "No, Justin, they were mad at you because you were being an asshole." I didn't respond at first; I thought maybe Danny hadn't seen something or was confused. I started to explain, and he stopped me again, reiterating that he knew what had happened and that I was an asshole. That next hour was one of my first lessons in life as an adult. Luckily for me, it came from someone who had both my respect and attention. In no particular order, I learned the following:

1. Of course, I was the asshole. I was giving their food away without asking, nor was I considered that to survive at a sawmill for two weeks at a time without a car was hard and that resources were precious.

2. I had insulted them by suggesting I had been buying them food so they didn't have to eat the food they specifically picked for themselves. Somehow I knew what they liked more than they did.

3. I never told them the extra food was for them, and they would have feared touching it to upset the owner and find themselves out of a job and a place to stay. They would have let it rot while they went hungry before stealing something that wasn't theirs.

4. In their mind, I had already insulted the boss by having

boots as lovely as his and then bragging about it. In their world, I had humiliated Ray right in front of them. Plus, I insulted them by flippantly purchasing both the original and replacement boots more minor than a week later, representing an entire week's worth of wages and untold difficulty getting to a proper boot store.

5. Because I rode with Danny every day, they already felt threatened and extra responsible for my safety above their own. They had been modifying the way they usually did jobs to make them easier on me. For me, disrespecting them after taking on extra work because of me was double or triple insulting.

6. In my fucked-up privileged way, I had assumed they could read, and while Clifford could, Johnny nor his son could read well. That explained why despite needing one every day, neither used a tape measure. Instead, they would use a guide stick with pre-marked intervals because they couldn't read a tape. Even if I had—which I hadn't—written a note on the extra food, it wouldn't have mattered. I had only looked at the entire thing from my perspective in my ignorance.

7. I had also failed to realize just how different my life was compared to theirs. There was nothing inherently bad or wrong about mine being different. Where I erred was in failing to acknowledge someone else's life might have been different than my own. That translated to arrogance and a flippant air that tainted every other aspect of our interactions.

This arrogance on my part showed just how much of a kid I still was. This truth was, in some ways, subtle and unspoken but so obvious and loud at the same time. I had acted as if that truth didn't exist, and it indeed did.

Over the next few months, I worked to change some of my behaviors and rebuild trust with the sawmill crew. Over time, I learned how to handle the food situation. I first replaced the potted meat I had fed to the dog with a six-pack of the same stuff. I first considered an entire case of the potted meat but thought about how it might be received. I initially stopped bringing extra food each day. At the end of the week resorted to saying my Granny had bought too much of whatever lunchmeat and it needed to get used before it went bad. It wasn't offered in charity but instead its acceptance was asked in service so they could help me use it before it spoiled. It didn't matter that it had a purchased on date right on the package or that my Granny was dead. I resolved to work just as hard and as long as they did, to never take a break or let them divide jobs. I didn't mind sharing the same tasks, but there was no more of them doing the hard part while I did the easy part. The weeks immediately after the food incident was brutal, without a doubt. They were some mean and tough "sum bitches" that could outwork an athlete in his prime.

From the day of the talk with Danny, I made a personal effort to be more present and observant of details for clues when I could. I would find out the knives they used with the dark-red handles were Case "Granddaddy" knives which went out of production in the late '60s. It is possible they were indeed given to those men by their granddaddies. When new, they were one of the most expensive knives you could have bought from the Case catalog and likely represented a cherished object to whoever carried them. They would choose to use their fingers rather than risk dirtying up a prized possession—it wasn't bad manners; it was respect.

I also learned that none of the men were homeless and that Johnny and Clarence both had cars. They chose to stay up at the mill so that they didn't waste the cost of fuel and travel. They had found camping at the mill allowed them to save even more money to send back to their families each month, and that's why no matter what, they would go back at least once a month to take the money they had made that month to their families.

I'm not sure who's the idea was, but at some point, it was decided to work at the mill for a year meant until the end of the calendar year. As it turned out, the same boards that let light in also didn't stop much wind either. As winter came, the work was frigid and painful. A large portion of the business came from making railroad ties for the Mexican government. One day though, the Mexican government decided they didn't like our railroad ties anymore, and the only thing going out the door were pallets and logs for resale. Two the business, In which I added little additional value. By New Year's of 1998, I had already started to plan for my next adventure, which was only possible because of the lessons I learned working those nine months in Ghent, KY.

Darrell inspired the next adventure, and he didn't even know it. I had always been willing to explore what it would take to have my own business, just like him. I look back and see him with a genuine business open to the public while he was in high school as something that served to normalize the concept to me. Starting your own business is something people often aspire to do "one day" or after they get some money saved, but Darrell did it while he was in high school. If he could make it work, why couldn't I? Following him, I had selected a business that revolved around a hobby I already enjoyed. While RC cars were fantastic and definitely on the list, I instead decided to do a paintball store. My friends and I played paintball quite a bit, and since I was the only one with a full-time income, I often found myself footing a substantial portion of the bill for our play. To reduce this cost, I had first explored what it would take to fill my CO2 tanks and then buy the ammunition from a wholesale source. I quickly identified significant markups and identified my hobby as something that could be a big business.

As I get started, I want to premise the following few chapters. Teenage years are like dog years because while they only take a single calendar year, they seem to occupy so much more space in terms of memories. They are also very rose-colored—that is to say, a found teenage memory, when viewed in the harsh light of reality, often does not maintain the same glow. Paint-ball and its associated journey take several years to play out from beginning to end. Having lived it, I would say it feels even longer. That period is also a time in my life that was somewhat distorted between my actual reality and what I was telling myself. I'm not talking about gross inaccuracies—if it makes it into this book, it either happened or, at the very least, my perspective of it had happened. I am talking about the difference between a successful enterprise from the perspective of a seventeen-year-old based solely on the size of deposits in a bank account versus actual, objective measurements of revenue and margins made in hindsight by a financial professional who evaluates business for a living. When I write about my experiences with paintball, I use the context I had at that time. If I identify a perspective by looking backward, I use the context I have now as a professional.

Having identified the opportunity that was paintball, I started to do some homework on just what it would take to make a store a reality. One of the first things I did was research the local competition and see what else was there. I found three competitors in my exhaustive research—which included a good old-fashioned phone book. Over the next year, I would find I had missed two partial competitors, one who only rented equipment and one who only offered equipment for order through a regular gun store. I made it my business to visit every competitor I could. One was housed in a room attached to an old barn visible from the highway. They offered rental and sales with a modest selection of equipment. His space was unimpressive in size, but he and his wife ran a good business. From that time, of all of my competitors, he is the only one still in business today.

Looking back (real perspective), I didn't make an excellent impression. When I did talk to him, I have heard I was bold and matter-of-fact, stating I was going to have way more of a selection, better prices, etc. As an adult, if someone like that came into my store, I would have happily shown him the door. The next store was an army-navy surplus store that also sold paintball gear. Their selection was minimal and what they sold was simply a sideline to their primary business. Looking back, this would still be a fair summary of their operation. The final store was a paintball-only retail store in a strip center. At the time, I remember it as being a little out of the way but not bad. It was in a busy part of town, but you had to know where to find it. It was run by a husband-and-wife team who might have had a passing interest in the sport but certainly didn't seem to be in a position to be actively involved. The husband did indeed participate in the full-scale woods events, and I suspect their location selection was made in a conscious compromise of cost and visibility that made sense for them. Their shop continued for another few years but also eventually closed.

Having determined the competition was lacking for one reason or another, my decision was made. I then set out to find a wholesale supplier, of which there were precisely two—PMI and National Paintball. In the years leading up to my involvement, there had been some previous consolidation of the suppliers. Still, the two-party dynamic existed for the entirety of my run, with the occasional direct-from-manufacture products leveling the field. Both suppliers required minimum initial order sizes that were about the same. Only one required you have a business license, certificate of insurance, and actual store with a sign requiring a picture as proof. The other was simply happy to take your money. Can you guess which one seventeen-year-old me chose? I went with the easy one. There were pros and cons to each, but I still think I chose the right one from a growth and learning perspective. However, the willingness to create new competition for existing customers should have been a red flag. After a single phone call expressing my interest, I was signed up, and a package arrived a week later. It had stickers, a t-shirt, catalogs, and a wholesale price list. I carefully went through the entire product line and came up with what I wanted my first batch of inventory to look like. As instructed, I sent this list back to them and got my final quote. As it was a "big order," my sales rep, Anthony, gave me a bigger discount than usual. They had almost everything I ordered in stock and just needed a cashier's check for nine thousand four hundred dollars.

That wasn't that much of a surprise as I had run the numbers using the price list and thought it would be just over ten thousand dollars to get started. I had about thirty-four hundred dollars saved up from working and had a plan to get the rest. I was going to get it from Papaw. As far as I was concerned, he was rich, and I only needed about the same amount it would cost for tuition had I gone back to the private school. Not desiring to write a blank check but acknowledging the level of real work I had put in at the sawmill and with the business planning, he agreed to go to the bank with me. At the bank, we met with one of his friends, the bank's president. Hollis was a matter-of-fact gentleman, and while not amused with a seventeen-year-old coming to him asking for a loan, he was willing to listen and even review the carefully handwritten business plan, complete with lists and charts I glued on with rubber cement. Hollis had questioned my assumptions and said that if I only borrowed the sixty-four hundred dollars I was asking for, even with my funds, I would essentially be bankrupt immediately after making my first purchase. He also asked who I would use to help with the books and if we had incorporated yet. As I didn't have good answers to either of those questions, he assisted me in deciding that we needed to incorporate asap, and we agreed that Papaw's tax guy would be a suitable bookkeeper. When it came to the amount to borrow, he made it easy. He let me have a credit line of ten thousand dollars, and the interest was ten percent for whatever amount was outstanding. He knew the rate was high, but he hoped it would motivate me to pay it back quickly.

Looking back, I was scammed, but not in the wrong way. The bank was going to loan me the money because Papaw was a good customer, and the money would be leaving his account one way or another, and they knew that. Hollis had the forethought to treat me with dignity and tried to teach me something about how all of this worked. He picked ten percent because it was easy for me to understand and still cheaper than a credit card. The selection of ten thousand dollars was two-fold. Yes, I did indeed need more capital than I had anticipated, and that was one lesson, but the other was it cost the same amount of paperwork and effort to set up a small or large credit line, but the interest payments on large ones are much higher. Therefore, it was a way of making the loan worth it to the bank in the first place. Lastly, Hollis didn't give the business the loan, as I was only seventeen, and we hadn't incorporated yet; it was in Papaw's name. So, in reality, he gave Papaw—who had many hundreds of thousands of dollars with the bank—a ten-thousand-dollar line of credit at ten percent interest with a personal guarantee. Not very risky, but an excellent way to build a business. There was only one businessman in the room that day, and it wasn't Papaw or me.

Ecstatic with the news, I let my supplier know they could ship the items cash on delivery (COD), and I'd give the check to the UPS guy. I cleaned out an extra closet as I was just going to operate out of the house until I got enough business to open an actual store. I planned to take my gear to different games each weekend and sell out of my truck to get enough business to open a store. I was well on the way despite having already made a few big mistakes like ordering an inventory of super expensive tournament-level guns that were too expensive for the average player. I chose them because they were flashy and what I wanted personally, not because I thought they would be easy to sell, which was a huge mistake that would take almost a year to remedy. Looking back, I thought my sales rep's understanding that I was opening a store would have helped me choose a better inventory mix. Still, I suspect he was simply happy to get the ultra-expensive, slow-moving items off his shelves, and that's why he made me such a "great deal."

Regardless of the missteps, I was on my way to legitimately owning and running a paintball store that, even by my adult standards, would be successful. I had just turned seventeen, and it was going to be a bumpy road, but at least for the first time in a few years, I had a path, no matter how rough

Chapter 9

Waking up While Riding In a Car and Only Thinking of Death

Despite its humble beginnings, the paintball store had been doing well. After just a few months of mobile operations, I secured my first physical location. It was a small building that had been a country store in the past. It was about 450 square feet and cost me four hundred dollars a month. I decorated and finished the space myself. I installed carpet tiles and pegboard, painted the walls, and even built a workbench/counter area next to a secondhand display case I had found. I had settled on the name Splat City and had business cards, and a large outdoor banner made up that I hung from the wall on the outside of the building. I had expanded into equipment rentals and timed the Christmas rush perfectly, selling the last gun in my inventory the night before Christmas.

Each month's sales increased, and by the sixth month in business, I was selling almost twenty thousand dollars of new stuff every month. I had a credit card machine, a point-of-sale system, everything. My total fixed overhead was less than six hundred dollars, and I wasn't even taking a salary. I was operating off a margin that seemed decent for me at the time and had about fifty thousand in profits saved from that first ten-thousand-dollar credit line. Looking back on things, the margin wasn't enough at only around twenty-seven percent combined across all lines but was workable. I hadn't cleared the credit line, so I was only sitting on forty, not fifty, but it was still real profit and looked sustainable. The sales of C02 and the guns' rental were where the real money was, making up only fifty percent of total sales but accounting for nearly eighty percent of the profit. These numbers aren't sexy or fun and never make it into the glamorous versions of my story.

Emboldened by easy success and being only seventeen led to me being incredibly self-assured. I could do no wrong in my mind, and any warning or advice that came my way was quickly discarded. My next big idea was that I wanted to expand. I didn't just want a better store—which was part of it—but I wanted more than just a store. At least I did after talking to a persuasive commercial real estate agent. He talked me into/I talked myself into looking for a space I could turn into an indoor arena. The first location I had settled on was going to be a new seventy thousand square foot family fun center with both an RC car racetrack and an indoor paintball arena. At about ½ the size of a Walmart, it would feature two stores, party rooms, a warehouse for storage, and more. Surprisingly, no bank wanted anything to do with loaning money on a three-million-dollar building topped with another quarter million in improvements for a seventeen-year-old entrepreneur with five months of moderate success.

The realtor's next option was a more modest thirty thousand square foot lease costing only seven thousand dollars per month. It had space for an arena and a nice showroom complete with bathrooms and a counter area that would be converted into a concession stand. For all the positives, it also had a few negatives. The arena area wasn't heated or cooled. It also had little to no natural light, so to see inside, you had to turn lights on, and they were the old-fashioned high-pressure sodium ones that ate electricity.

Looking back on this decision, I am conflicted. Please make no mistake about it; somebody with some sense should have said NOOOOOOO. But I do understand why no one did. I had been successful until that point, not just from a gross sales perspective but also in real profit. While expensive, the cost related to a lease wasn't impossible and could have even been covered at a push using just the sales from the old location. It was reasonable to expect both sales and rentals to increase with the new site and a new revenue stream to be added from the arena entry fees. But—and this is a huge BUT—all of this potentially positive and good news is dwarfed by increased operating cost, staff, insurance, and capital improvement costs. I had failed to account for any of that real business stuff, and that's why it was a bad idea.

Regardless of something being a good or bad idea, I signed the lease and was ready to make a move. Before we could open at the new location, I had one last thing to take care of—changing the name. A very sleazy and slippery local paintball scumbag came to me with a scam that even at the time seemed like bullshit, but he played me just right. He had told me about another store that used the name Splat City and that they were going to sue me if I opened an arena under that name blah, blah, blah. I think he was looking to squeeze me for money, but being the asshole kid that I was, I said fuck-em and changed the name that day to American Paintball Games, or APG for short. From my perspective, it was a better name and was listed sooner in the phone book than the competition, which still mattered back then. That slimy guy was trying to shake me down for money; he was such as scum bag. I learned later that he had helped the other store using the same name set up their vendor account with PMI using pictures of my store and signage once I moved out, essentially assuming my abandoned business identity. They eventually had a tiny store with kiddie cages for their kids in the corner and the dirtiest, grimiest arena I've ever seen. Unfortunately, scum bags and scams would be a constant threat in the years to come.

It was all hands were on deck once we started working at the new arena. I hadn't been savvy enough to negotiate starting the lease payments only once improvements were completed or even having the upgrades included in the cost of the lease. Those would have been actual business moves, but at this point,

I was still just pretending to be a businessman. Every day we didn't open it cost me $230.13. I had that amount as a ticking clock over me—tick, tock, tick, tock. Just before I signed the lease for the arena, I had also decided to take tax advice from an idiot. The advice pertained to taxes I did not even owe, but I suspect I just wanted the excuse. I bought a nice truck—a true beast of a truck—a 1997 Hummer H1 convertible in competition yellow with a black convertible top. It was the same sort of truck Arnold Schwarzenegger drove. Garish and loud, it was a perfect and excellent use of about seventy-five thousand dollars plus tax. Not having that kind of money lying around with the arena renovations in full swing, I was able to finance it for the low price of fifteen hundred dollars per month in 1998. There was some logic behind this purchase as it also served as a rolling billboard, and it did indeed do a particularly excellent job at that. It was also now my daily transportation, as up until that point, I would occasionally drive a project Mustang around or borrow a car from Papaw.

Despite the challenges, I had the arena open in just over a month. I was tapped out financially and emotionally but recovering on both fronts as we again had quick success. Sales were as strong as ever, and the arena was a big hit. However, we had added quite a bit of overhead—not just in a more extensive lease, but in the form of insurance and payroll, as I could no longer run the operations myself. I had first tapped friends and acquaintances to help run things, but after a few false starts, I resorted to more professional options.

Looking back, this phase was also a turning point. I once again had pulled off a miracle by securing some success despite increasing negative pressures. From my current perspective, I had run into a situation that I can identify as an operating income crunch that would last for several months. Seventeen-year-old me instead mistook it for a need for a one-time capitalization event in which if I could get a new batch of inventory to restock everything so, all would be well. Papaw to the rescue. He had recently enjoyed the run of perceived success himself and even got a new money manager to help him invest his money for better returns. Lucky for seventeen-year-old me, American Paintball was just what the manager needed to justify fees and commissions on withdrawals. By the summer of '98, I had completed two capital bailouts disguised as investments. The two payments totaled about a hundred grand, and combined with the typical churn of the store and arena; it looked good on paper. If you just ignored where the money came from and the potential recurring nature of the problem, things were fixed and looking great going forward.

New money in hand, shelves stocked, and the bleeding slowed, operations started to settle into a good rhythm. I had a real, full-time manager, Eric, running things. His only complaint was that I still hadn't set an official salary for myself, and I used the till as my bank account. Just as he would have a good night, I would stroll in before the deposit and grab my share. Over time, he slowly dragged me to a more disciplined approach, and by the summer, he had me taking a regular paycheck. I had bought another car, this time a more practical race car for the street as the Hummer was just too big to drive every day. I had moved out of Papaw's house into my Mom's old house. She had moved out once she separated from her husband, Rick. Agreeing to pay the meager mortgage payment, it was all mine. I proceeded to turn that house into the bachelor pad you would expect for a newly independent seventeen-year-old with all the free cash in the world. I was experiencing some success, and the new store had also turned a corner falling solidly into the black.

By the end of the summer in 1998, we turned a real profit, albeit meager. We had a pile of debt to get rid of, but if we could make it through the fall and keep demand up for products and the arena, we would be doing something. To get ready for this, I was making a special trip up to our supplier in Jersey. I wanted to see what new products were out and available to fill the cases. I was also on a mission to negotiate terms for the extension of credit to buy paintballs in bulk. I'm talking full semi-truck quantities. This larger volume would help me lock in a little more margin on my lowest profit but highest volume product. This prospect was all the more tempting when I might be able to do it using the supplier's money and not my own.

I never flew to New Jersey to visit the suppliers. I suppose it was because I always intended on bringing lots of stuff back, and by that point, it had become routine to drive. It was a long trip, covering six hundred miles and eleven hours. It was always done in teams straight through; that time, it was Papaw and me. We left on a Monday night—they were always the slowest days at the shop so that I wouldn't be missed. On Tuesday, we met with the supply house owner and made substantial progress on the terms. He would allow us to have about half of what we wanted on credit that fall as long as we kept our order volume up. The supplier didn't want to be trading tomorrow's sales for sales today; they wanted to see us keep growing. It wasn't a perfect deal, but it worked, I had talked with Papaw, and he was willing to put the other half in, no questions asked. I cleaned out the display cases of anything unique or cool and had those items packed up. All of the purchases fit in the car's trunk—a 1995 Cobra R Mustang. Not exactly the best road trip car, but it was what I was driving at that point, having tired of the giant Hummer.

Other than discussing the terms during the meeting, the only other thing of note was that I was introduced to airsoft, a cross between BB guns and paintball using small, plastic BBs. They said it was going to be huge, but I was skeptical. Papaw thought it was great, and I suppose we considered the options for having designated times for both sports that coming fall as they could both be played in the current arena with slight modifications. Agreeing to revisit the airsoft discussion later, we got on the road and promptly hit Philadelphia traffic. That traffic added a good hour or more to our trip, extending our return home to around 3 a.m. the following day. It was a rather unremarkable trip across the turnpike. Papaw drove as I managed to get a speeding ticket on the way up the night before, and we didn't want to shoot for a two-for-one special that trip. I faded off and fell asleep somewhere around the middle of Pennsylvania.

I would consider myself a spiritual person now, but that faith has grown since having a family and children. In 1998, I was a believer, but generally, I was much less spiritual than I am now. I only bring these facts up as a way to preference or base what I am about to describe. I was sleeping in the car and awoke suddenly; startled, I immediately grabbed the steering wheel from the passenger's seat. The car swerved violently as Papaw wrestled the wheel back away from me. For him, it must have been quite an experience to have me wake up from a sound sleep and, in one swift motion, try to grab the wheel out of his hands. It's a wonder we didn't wreck or worse. It took just a moment for me to regain my composure. At that moment, the feeling I had was the same as when you're startled awake by the alarm clock during a profound sleep—dizzy, lost, and confused; the feeling passes pretty quick, and you fully absorb you were dreaming. It was a lot like that, but it was different—this had another component.

What I was dreaming about—or, more accurately, what my vision was—involved the most visual personification of death you can imagine. There were rotting corpses with their skeletons laid partially bare. There were skulls with their flesh dripping off in long, drippy, waxy strings, somewhere between rotting and melting. The intense colors of red and a particular shade of brown I have since come to be familiar with were, before that moment, unknown to me. There were sounds and smells, but I can only describe them as being more than one sound at once and more than one smell at once—combined but still distinct. I was overstimulated, but instead of everything being blocked out in the chaos, everything was infinitely separable and precise. Imagine a football stadium filled with rotting corpses and bodies and seeing the entire stadium full and every individual occupant simultaneously. At the same time as the macabre and visceral imagery, there weren't any other things you might otherwise associate with that sort of imagery in a religious context:

no devils, no fire, no sense of fear or despair. What I saw can only be described as death—that's the only single word that covers it—but if you used a thousand different words together, you couldn't capture it all. I woke up afraid and scared because of what I had seen. I wasn't afraid of the images; it wasn't fear the images represented—it was fear on my part because I had seen them, I had seen death.

I'm not sure if it was a glitch in the matrix or divine providence that woke me up at just that point in time. Maybe by waking up and grabbing the wheel, I set some butterfly effect or series of events that would forever change me. If I had put into motion some cosmic series of events, I couldn't have known on the lonely road just outside of Wheeling, West Virgina, crossing into Ohio at **11:30 p.m. on August 18th, 1998,** what that series of events might have been or what they would look like. Regardless of what was set in motion or had transpired, the timing was not insignificant.

We arrived back in Kentucky that even right on time, and I immediately went to bed, planning on going to the store early that morning. What I remember seeing came to mind once more but quickly faded away. Over the next week or so, life at the shop went well. Nothing out of the ordinary, just general stuff. That weekend, Eric and I had stayed late while he closed up. He had been talking to a girl who worked across the street at the pizza place, and we decided to try to get a double date set up. I knew another girl who worked there from my days back at the Y and thought it might be worth a shot. We set the double date up for that Wednesday when both the girls were off. Eric brought the booze as he was old enough to buy. We started the night with the girls arriving fifteen to twenty minutes earlier. It was dark out, and after the store had closed, so I guess about 9:30 – 10 p.m. based on the time of year. Just after they arrived, I heard a knock at the front door. That was unusual because no one ever used it, although it was the front door. There wasn't even a sidewalk leading to the front as the driveway, and the main entrance was around the back. I looked out the window, and I could see a cop car—or at least it looked like one, maybe it was unmarked. I prepared my best Eddie Haskel impression and opened the door, ready to address an inevitable noise or a party complaint.

I opened the door, and it was a cop and another guy dressed in a sports coat. They asked if I knew Katy White, and I responded that I did, and she was my Mother, but she didn't live here anymore. I assumed she had gotten involved in some check scheme or trouble over drugs; just as I was about to disavow her and anything she was possibly involved with, the guy in the sports coat spoke up. The gentleman said he was sorry to inform me but that she had been found dead that evening. My reaction was muted—or at least in some way unusual—and the only explanation I could give was that maybe I had been in shock. My reaction was reserved enough for the officer to say, "You don't seem very upset about that." I responded that I was upset, but there had just been a lot of things between us over the years. They had a few questions, like when was the last time, I saw her and who she usually hung out with but nothing detailed. They gave me their cards and said I needed to come down and identify the body the next day at a specific address. At that time, the officers didn't have much in the way of detail—either they weren't sharing or didn't know them. Completely ignoring my guest and my machismo, I started to cry as soon as I closed the door. I called Papaw and told him over the phone, but it was almost as if he didn't believe me. His house was only a few miles away, and I made the trip in a few minutes to redeliver the news in person. That night we cried and held each other; the only solace we could find was that she was finally back with her mom and brother.

The next day was filled with misery and hassle for me. I had gone down to the address the detectives had given me, explaining to the front desk attendant at the hospital that my Mom had died and I needed to identify her. Either I misunderstood the task or took down the wrong address because I spent the next two hours shuffled between different orderlies and morgue attendants looking at the corpses of dead grandmas instead of my Mom. Somehow in the confusion of things, my uncle Donny managed to be contacted by either the police or someone else and officially identified the body. I eventually got a hold of the detective again that following day and understood better the circumstances of how she had been found. The neighbors had grown concerned over not seeing her for what turned out to be over a week. They had noticed her car sitting in the driveway and may have even noticed a smell at some point. Someone went to check on her and reported seeing a black person slumped over the couch through a window. Police came and started the investigation. It is possible they initially didn't think the body was of my Mom, and that's why they wanted someone to identify her despite the police having her ID and other identification available to them. The coroner would place her time of death more than a week before they found her body, and that would have been just a day or two before her electricity was disconnected for nonpayment. In the August sun, her body sat in an un-air conditioned trailer home for more than a week before someone found her. That was why her skin had darkened, and she was confused for a black woman.

I made up for whatever indignity she had in death with the celebration of her life at the funeral. She had somewhat prophetically communicated to others in casual conversation just a few weeks earlier that she wanted to be cremated when she died. I took this into advice and had her cremated per her wishes. She got the best wooden box they had to place her ashes in. We buried the ashes in a vault with a headstone next to her Mother and Brother. She shares the same shade of the dogwood tree that they do every summer afternoon. My Mother was the best Mom she could be. Many struggles and trauma helped make her the person she would be most of her life, but that wasn't her whole story. She was also beautiful and intelligent, loving and sweet. You didn't get to see as much of that as you wanted, but it was still there. Before her death, our relationship had improved. It hadn't been repaired fully, but it was better. I lived in her old house; the one Papaw rehabbed for her. She had moved out a few years before getting away from memories or a persistent lack of a driver's license, which was complicated by living just a block from the police station. We would occasionally talk, and I remember one of the happiest moments in my life being when she and Rick stopped up at the paintball store on a busy day. I made them feel like kings and gave the entire tour, even introducing them to staff and friends.

She got to see me as successful and strong on my home turf. Her little man had turned into a man at that point, and she was happy, maybe even a little bit relieved that some of her bullshit hadn't messed me up too bad. This also reminds me that you can't have happiness without sorrow. My biggest regret in life is the following—I am sharing this to be accurate and warn anyone who has malice in their hearts to ignore it when it comes to your parents, no matter how hard it is. My last memory of my Mother alive came a few weeks before she died. She had called the store a few times trying to get a hold of me. No one would give her my cell phone number based on prior instructions. One day, I finally got caught, and she got me on the phone. She told me her deck outside of her trailer had rotten boards, and she was afraid she would fall through them. I headed over to see her that afternoon, expecting to see a dilapidated deck in serious need of repair. While not expecting to see a full emergency, I did expect some level of damage, and I had already put a crew on hold in case the deck needed to be replaced.

I got to the house, and we visited. She shared her displeasure with it being hard to get a hold of me which on my part was by design. That started some mild tension, but nothing I hadn't dealt with before. We then proceed to look at her deck. There was nothing wrong with it—it was dirty and had some algae growing near the edges, but it was in fine shape. I exploded on her, yelled, and accused her of wasting my precious time. We argued as I was getting back into my truck, and I began to pull out of her driveway. As one last fuck-you to her and to teach her a lesson about wasting my precious time with her made-up deck problems I proceeded to run over her mailbox with my truck—the giant military-sized Hummer. I went back and forth, back and forth ten times or more, turning her mailbox into a flat banana of scrap steel. She watched me, and I looked her in the eyes as I pulled away. That was the last time I saw my Mom in person. I believe we spoke once more briefly, where I gave her a half-ass apology, but that was the last time I looked into her eyes, and I was breaking her heart while I was doing it.

As an adult with my children, I now know what was really going on. She had missed me and wanted to see me and desperately spend time with me. She didn't know how to say that or get me to listen to her request. She knew she didn't need the deck fixed. Instead, she just wanted to talk to me. This regret of mine is persistent and one I have tried to get others to avoid from the experience of just how bad it can be. Some have listened, and some haven't, with devastating consequences. You never know when your last conversation with someone will be—don't let it end like I did mine.

Mary Katheryn "Katy" White was born on July 6th, 1960, and died in the late evening of August 18th, 1998, at thirty-eight years old. Katy was three years younger than I was when I sat writing this book. She was a mother, a daughter, a sister, a wife, and an aunt. She was an artist and a nurse. She was a lover and a fighter—sometimes both at the same time. But most of all, she was just unapologetically my **MOM**, and she will forever be missed.

Chapter 10

Barn Fires and My First Highspeed Chase

It's 3:30 in the morning on Thursday night in the summer of 1998. Two shadowy figures are walking around inside the paintball arena. The lights are off, and the place has been closed for hours. Are they breaking in, or are they stealing stuff? One of the figures crouches down and starts to mess with one of the arcade games in the area just outside of the arena. He is crawling, and under the dash area of the Daytona racer arcade game like he's trying to hot-wire it or something. The other figure hands him a tool—something long and skinny like a Slim Jim. There's a bang, and suddenly the machine comes to life, first one screen and then the other right next to it. The two figures sit down and play those games until daylight, never stopping to put another quarter in. It was 6:30 the next day when Darrell and I stopped playing those games. Our eyes were bloodshot—more than tweaker hopped up on trucker aspirin. And yes, I did hot-wire them—or, more accurately, found a way to press the "test" button on the inside through a tiny gap at the edge of the case. Every button press was equivalent to inserting a dollar, so forty to fifty should have probably done the trick.

This and things like it had become commonplace for Darrell and me. We spent at least some time together every day. Sometimes it was a few hours after he got off work, messing around with a race-car in the shop. We had set up what was a race shop in the barn behind Darrell's house. It was a sizable thirty-by-forty affair with tall ceilings and a concrete floor. My budget was a little larger than his, but his skill set and patience exceeded mine. We had drag cars, race engines, off road trucks, rail buggies—you name it, we had it. There was even an alcohol drag boat parked next to the barn for a while. We shared tools, supplies, parts, and vehicles as one. What was mine was his, and what was his was mine. This communal enjoyment was only possible with two best friends like us. We would spend hours together and alone in the shop. As my schedule was slanted to nights, I would often spend the early morning hours after the arena closed deep into the following day working on cars. Sometimes Darrell and I would pass in the morning as he was leaving for work and I was heading to bed. The only rules about the garage and cars were not to start the loud vehicles after dark, disturb Darrell's mom, and not let other people see what we had inside.

When we weren't working on cars, playing video games, frog gigging, or just driving; we talked about life, girls, what exotic cars were the most remarkable—pretty much anything. We also managed to find a way to relive events that had only happened a few years prior, much the same way old-timers talk about the good ole days when sitting at the bar.

His style remained the same, never aging or adapting as time went on. Darrell still wore white t-shirts and jeans. The mullet had grown a little longer, and the sunglasses were discontinued, so he was stuck with the next newest model. His mannerisms never changed, and he was teaching his signature "whoooooooooo" to an even wider audience with it becoming quite the trend at local hangouts and bars. The only thing that changed about Darrell in the prior three years was that he had gotten a new truck and a new girlfriend. He was fond of both. He kept that truck for almost ten years, but he has held the girlfriend for nearly twenty-five years. He now calls her wife. They have three beautiful girls—two like her and one exactly like him, signature "whooooo" and all.

While there were undoubtedly distractions such as work and girls, we always seemed to make time for each other. Part of this was out of a duty or obligation to each other. We had been through enough at that point. We were karmically connected between my kidnappings, numerous beatings, and my mom's death. The other part of it was that we learned from each other. He taught me about people and life, how to make a deal, and how to read a room. I taught him about fast cars and how to make the best out of shitty situations. He was an inspiration and a mentor to me, and he was the one that helped me know I was able to start my own business.

I had always viewed Darrell as the most intelligent guy I knew. He was far more intelligent than me or others I knew who had gone to college and graduated. Darrell never graduated college, but he went for a while and had excellent grades. His choice to stop was strictly practical and held to this day. To Darrell, spending the $50,000 on the school would never do anything for him that spending the same amount on something real wouldn't. He had always planned on working for himself, and since he wasn't asking for his degree to give himself the job, it wasn't a good use of the money. Instead, he spent his money on his share of the sawmill, which he owns.

When I was on the verge of tough decisions, he always stood on the side, telling me what he thought. Despite being willing to tell me the truth and give me honest opinions, he never punished me for not taking his advice. He never sat back and said I told you so. That just wasn't the kind of guy he was. He didn't want me to do the arena at the paintball store—and he was right, but that didn't mean he rubbed it in my face when things got hard. Instead, Darrell brainstormed and struggled with me, partly trying to help and reminding me I didn't have to do it alone. Darrell's home life was good. He understood the Appalachian dynamic with the drama and the enhanced roles everyone played. Fortunately for Darrell, his particular flavor was better adjusted and stable. I used to get a little jealous of what he had in that regard, that somehow it was just a little better than mine. Instead of rubbing that in my face, he shared it. There was a point where I could count on a supper plate being set for me at their table every day. His Mom would ask me about school and later work—not out of courtesy but because she cared.

Not content to just be best friends and hang around, Darrell and I started planning some adventures. We had always done this on a small scale, like camping trips and off road trails, but we wanted more. That year, we had two big trips planned for opposite parts of the country and times of the year. I had signed up for the Hummer Challenge that summer—it was an off-road race through the Florida Everglades using Hummers to navigate certain checkpoints. He was going to be my navigator and partner. There would be challenges the team had to complete at each checkpoint before moving on. It was modeled after the Camel Trophy, a similar event for Land Rovers. This was to be part road rally and part basic training.

The winter trip was to the Upper Peninsula of Michigan for a week of snowmobiling Papaw had always taken those trips with his buddies. Darrell and I always heard the stores and thought what a better adventure it could be. I had even managed a snowmobile trip with Papaw one year just before Granny died, and it was terrific. Despite being fraught with breakdowns, severe weather, and illness, that trip remains one of my best memories. Learning from the previous mistakes, our trip would involve driving up and renting sleds there so we could guarantee good days of riding. 1998 had been a tough year, culminating with the loss of my mom, but it wasn't all bad. I had the Hummer race coming up, a new girlfriend, and I had managed to squeak out an OK summer with the store. To celebrate that marginal success I bought yet another Hummer, this time a green wagon model with even bigger tires and a full compliment of off road lights and guards. If I had learned anything in life until that point, it should have been that things could change instantly, and with a phone call to the store in September of 1998, things certainly changed.

I had stopped in the store to check on things while running errands around town. I was getting ready to leave in two days for The Hummer Challenge. I had finished the last tweaks to the truck that morning and needed to finish up securing the camping supplies. Most of the participants in the challenge were rich. They would be staying in delightful hotels at night after racing, sipping cocktails, and socializing. Not us. We had planned to camp at the racetrack and scout the route for the next day early.

On top of that, we were going to use a homemade tent. Remember I told you Ray, Darrell's dad, was a survival instructor? That's only part of it. He helped draft the book on survival used to train pilots. In homage to Ray, we had secured an army surplus parachute and a few long, wooden poles we were going to use to fashion our tent. Ray showed us how to split the ends of the cords to harvest the inner fibers and tie off the parachute to the poles so he could adjust the ventilation. We would be camping, but we were also doing so with grit. One of the last things we needed was a filled nitrogen tank to supply the impact gun on the truck. I had only planned on stopping for a minute at the paintball shop to fill the tank, and then I was heading back to the garage to finish up.

Just as I walked to the door, Jill handed me the phone and said it was Wallace, asking if I was hurt? Looking puzzled, I took the phone from her. What came next was a bizarre game. "Hey, where are you? You are not in the barn?" "Jason, you called me, and I am at the shop; where did you think I was? What are you talking about?" It took him a few seconds to regain cognitive function, and he said, "I was afraid you were in the barn. Your Hummer is on fire, and so is the barn." I hung up the phone and told Jill to call Papaw and tell him. I jumped in the car and raced out of the parking lot.

When I say raced, I mean race, the trip between the store and the barn covered the same road that was also the patch between my house and the store. That meant I had covered that same twisting and lunging two-lane, blacktop road four to eight times a day, every day, for three years. It's safe to say I knew the racetrack. It's also important to point out that my daily driver was a '95 Mustang Cobra R. The important part of the name is the "R"—it denotes race model, produced in a limited run of just twenty-five samples. You had to have a racing license to buy that 5.8 L beast from Ford. It had no radio, no heat, ac, or even a backseat. It was a race car for the street. Mine was modified with new heads and a supercharger, so it had around 550 HP, making it a 3000-pound handling and braking machine. I had previously gone as fast as 140 MPH on that road at night with no traffic. I suspect I went about the same speed that morning.

While not overtly reckless in my driving, it can only be called reckless to travel at those speeds on that road with traffic around. I am lucky I did not kill someone. By the time I had reached the two-thirds point of the trip, I had turned onto a larger, divided highway. Just then, I passed a cop. I'm not sure if he was responding to calls about my earlier driving or happened to notice my four-wheel drift of a right turn that I had just made. Either way, he spun around and was in hot pursuit. I saw the cop coming from the other direction and somehow wasn't surprised he had turned to pursue me. At that point, I decided to just drive to the fire and work it out later. I was only a few miles from the barn and in a high-speed chase with a cop close behind. He certainly wasn't gaining on me as his Crown Vic was outclassed. He could easily see my next turn because of the layout of the roads. About a hundred yards from Darrell's house, the traffic was stopped. You could see the smoke and flames and the fire trucks spraying water. Seeing the cop with his lights on maybe a quarter mile back, I pulled the car off the side onto the shoulder, ditching it while I ran towards the house. Through a small gap in the side yard, I went behind the house and ran up to the fire.

It seemed I caught some of the responders off guard and some might have even thought I had somehow come from out of the burning building as I emerged into view. I was suddenly stopped by firefighters, including the one who had called me. Maybe ten to fifteen seconds later, the sheriff came running up at nearly that same time Darrell's mom, Linda, came running up to me, crying and hugging me. It was all very emotional and, from the outside chaotic. It was that chaos that saved my bacon. There was significant confusion about whether I was actually in the barn when it caught on fire. People had seen me there maybe twenty to thirty minutes before and hadn't noticed I had driven the Mustang when I left. I came to the barn in the Hummer, and since they could see the Hummer, they assumed I was still there. That is why Wallace had called the store—not to tell me the barn was on fire but to tell someone else I had been hurt at the barn. I suspect the cop chasing me only got half this story and assumed I was rushing to the scene of a fire in which my loved one was believed to be inside.

Not a perfect excuse for running from the cops, but good enough. It was chaos between the first batch of firefighters, thinking I came out of the barn and the other bunch sorting out the cops and family. It was that chaos that led to the next few emotional events. Throughout the next thirty to forty-five minutes, with the fire still burning, I was reunited with Darrell's wife, Papaw, and Darrell. They all had gotten the word early on that there was a fire and no one could find me, which were both accurate statements. By the time the other truth about me being fine was known, they were very much on their way to the barn and unreachable as not everyone had cell phones. When they saw me, it was a relief that I wasn't dead, despite what their emotions and fear from the previous half-hour had been preparing them for. Nearly all of my memories of the immediate time around the fire are strongly affected by one or two emotions—the happiness I was alive and the fear I was dead.

The fire had been burning for maybe twenty to thirty minutes by the time I got there and burned just over an hour total. Given the amount of race gas, ammunition, compressed gas cylinders, and generally dangerous shit, it surprising it hadn't been for longer. When I first arrived, the entire structure of the barn was still standing, and while the Hummer was surrounded by fire, I didn't know it had indeed been on fire at that point. I believe I even implored the firefighters to pull it out by attaching a cable to the tow hitch and using the fire truck to pull it out. The explosions from acetylene tanks and a drum of race fuel quickly put an end to those thoughts.

That day, as soon as the flames were extinguished, we started assessing the losses. With the metal still hot, we clamored for a closer look, but every single item in the garage was a total loss. The vehicles lost or damaged included three Mustangs, a Hummer, two four-wheelers, and damage to a drag boat and an FJ-40 land cruiser. There were enough engines and parts to build two additional cars and a significant number of tools and equipment. There were a few firearms and maybe another twenty or thirty thousand dollars' worth of property belonging to others in one way or another. No matter how you sliced it, the losses were enormous. The one thing we didn't lose that day was each other. Despite all of the fear and emotion, I had died; that rumor had been greatly exaggerated through some miracle, and I was alive. It would be several days until I could start to process the events of that day and see them for the blessing they were.

I was still somehow more worried about stuff and things. How was I going to replace everything? As embarrassing as it is looking back, I knew I was safe in my decision to drive like an idiot to the fire, so what exactly was I rushing for? Did I expect to be able to save all my stuff if I could just get there quickly? I mean, it was asinine. I had risked myself and others so I could have a chance to be more upset about my shit as it was happening versus later? I have some theories as to why I acted that way at the time, but none of them are worth typing.

In the days after the fire, as we sorted through things, I have two overwhelming memories—a deep feeling this was all my fault and a sense of pending doom. The next few days were full of questions from the fire investigators. What did I remember seeing, what was I last doing, did I have any ideas about what happened, etc. They asked the same questions repeatedly. Every time I went through the questions, I gave them the same answers. I genuinely tried to be helpful and direct in every way.

Darrell also had questions. He was trying to understand how it happened as well. I went through nearly all the same answers with him. I say almost because his version had a slight change. I told him I stopped and grabbed an oil filter after leaving the barn that morning before stopping at the paintball shop. I had gone way earlier in the morning before ever getting to the barn. I somehow thought if he thought the fire started later after I left, he would hold me less responsible. That, of course, was bullshit as it was my fault as I had just left, and whether it caught fire five or twenty minutes after I left was essentially immediately after I left. There was another thing I hadn't talked to Darrel or the investigators about. It wasn't a fact in the traditional sense and didn't have actual relevance to the investigation, but it's what happened. When I left the barn that day, I had a bad feeling.

I was rushed, but I distinctly remember feeling uneasy to the point I even looked around and made sure things were OK before I left. I remember a slight smell of melted plastic, but I couldn't find anything despite looking. That wasn't surprising as I had been welding on a plastic-coated roof rack earlier, and the smell was powerful and very expected. I had only paused for a few seconds to glance around, nothing formal or diligent, just a half-assed looksee and a shoulder shrug. This is something I never told the investigators—not that it would have impacted their investigation—but it was indeed a detail I didn't tell them. The intuition of something being wrong nor my stretching of the period for Darrell affected the fire investigation one iota. But the investigation was just getting underway, and it would have consequences that reached way farther than a bad feeling.

In the event of plane and car crashes, something that often happens is somewhat peculiar. It's called object fixation, and it is when something's very presence causes all available attention and effort to be focused on it, even if that focus and concentration are at the cost of more impactful and helpful details. If a pilot is concentrated on altitude, they may intently watch the gauge and pull back on the stick, tickling the length higher and higher, only to completely forget about airspeed. They are in a full stall watching the altitude decrease as they fall to earth the next thing you know. Another example is how the flashing lights of emergency vehicles on the side of the road can draw drivers to them. They inadvertently draw the passing cars right into the obstacle by simply catching a driver's attention. I bring this up because it becomes relevant in the fire investigation. I am commenting on this from the perspective of then and now, having my formal training and experience with fire investigations as part of my job.

Both the fire department and the private fire investigator for the insurance company placed the cause of the fire on the Hummer—either from the fact I was welding on it or the insurance investigator's case from two shorted wires the had supposedly found. They were both wrong. The fire started somewhere near the back of the garage near the workbench where I had been using a set of torches to cut thin re-bar for tent pegs for the previous thirty to forty minutes. That information was shared with them—that I had been cutting outside and then went inside as the wind was making things difficult. I had made a lot of sparks once I moved inside, and while I did search at the time for embers, I didn't spray water or otherwise do more than a basic ruffle around. Just as I would only do the bare minimum when I left, I had just done the bare minimum when I provided only the most minimum of explanations.

It would have done no good to search for burn patterns or origin "V's" as the structure had been consumed, but the details and info were there. Instead, they were blinded by this big, green, shiny, different, and weird truck. They had never seen one in person, and since it was so thoroughly burned, the truck became their object fixation. They saw it and immediately misinterpreted every clue in a way to convince themselves it was the source of the fire. They ignored that it had an aluminum and fiberglass body that melts and even burns instead of a regular car. They forgot that this version was gasoline-powered and not diesel-like most Hummers, meaning its forty-five-gallon fuel tank affected the propagation significantly. They also ignored it was a civilian version with an entire interior covered in caret leather and plastic versus the bare-bones military version.

Things got more complicated for me—my moral failings combined with circumstance and perceptions to make a mess. While at the time I certainly felt the fire was my fault, remember I was also only seventeen. As a seventeen-year-old, it wasn't a stretch for me to think that the fire was my fault; I risked losing my best friend and what had essentially become my adopted family. Combine this with the fact that the investigators were happy to say it wasn't my fault but the Hummer's, and I was in quite the predicament. Then add two competing sets of adults who were wiser about the world's ways and knew that as long as everyone just let the insurance companies write checks to make everything better, everything would eventually work out and go away. No matter what happened, I was sure to lose—it was just a matter of when.

Things crept back to normal over the next several weeks and months, but it was different. Real tension was undoubtedly expected. It would get worse, sometimes with a comment and sometimes with a direct question that didn't have a good answer. No one wanted to hurt anyone's feelings, but no one wanted to be short-changed. Around that time, I was having dinner at Darrel's house one night, and while milling around the kitchen before Linda put the food out, I saw a stack of photos. I don't know who took the images, and I don't know if they were left out for me to see or if it was just luck. Either way, I could tell exactly what they were—photos of the torch-cut tent pegs, photos of the remnants of the torch set, pictures of the slag and cutting residue in the workbench area. They were photos that clearly showed the correct version of what happened to start the fire that day. At the time, I think I felt fear it would end badly once everybody knew I had screwed up and started the fire, which was obvious but somehow had slithered away from my consciousness. I was mad somehow; they didn't believe me when I said we would replace everything once the insurance company paid. And I was afraid for them because I had been led to believe that if the insurance company didn't pay, their coverage wouldn't be enough, and the only way to make them whole was to have our insurance pay.

Separate from what I believed to be fact was additional information I knew to be fact. I had too much pride to admit this openly to Darrell or anyone, but if my (Papaw's) insurance company didn't pay for everything, we would all be screwed because we didn't have the money to spend on our own. By the end of that next year, Papaw—and subsequently me—would be out of money and bankrupt with several hundred thousand dollars in debt by the following year. That was the definition of screwed up, and I could see it would not end well.

That complicated set of circumstances was further muddled by various other parties interjecting themselves with rumor and innuendo for their own gain. That only served to further drive the divide between our families and us. Our last argument started when someone asked if they could take some scrap parts off one of the Mustangs. As it was my Mustang, I said sure. However, it was apparent the person also needed to clear it with Darrell as they were on his property, and he hadn't been paid by insurance yet. I expected Darrell to say no—I was just too big of a pussy to tell the fat-ass who asked me no myself. The large fellow caused an even more significant problem. Darrell and I had nearly come to blows by the end of the day. It was clear I owed him money, that without the help of the insurance, I could not pay. It was also clear they were pursuing their insurance resolution away from ours that they were looking for us to make things right. I knew deep inside that we wouldn't make things right because we couldn't.

The last demand for payment came from Ray directly to Papaw, and it was for about fifty thousand, which looking back, seems about right. Papaw didn't pay, and I didn't pay; I didn't have the money, nor did Papaw, and even if we did, the damage had been done. The insurance company paid for the cars that had separate policies and the minimum limit for the "personal property" we had listed at the site garage. Darrell's insurance paid for the barn and some personal property but likely fell short of the due total. Papaw had cleared his conscious through a separate unrelated business deal with Danny about what was owed, but it's doubtful the money ever made it back to Ray and Darrell. I never could clear my consciousness of the events. About a year later, I had come across a neat Mustang that would make a good racecar and, through a mutual friend, arranged to purchase it and have it delivered to Darrell. The friend ended up taking credit for the car instead of giving it to me and, through that action, managed to remove himself from my friend's list.

I lost a great friend and a family over the barn fire. After that last fight, I didn't speak to Darrell for nearly fourteen years. He missed the birth of all three of my children, my marriage, and the death of Papaw. From what I can tell, I missed his marriage and the best, most exciting, and fun years of his life. Once I moved back to KY, I did write him a letter apologizing and fully taking responsibility for my role in the loss of the friendship and fire. We reconnected, and it was like we had only been gone from each other's lives for a few weeks in so many ways. We are a little older, but he still has a mullet, wears jeans and a white t-shirt, and can let out a rebel yell of "Whoooooooooo" with the best of them. I'm not as close with Linda and Ray as I once was, and I hate that, but I think that has a lot more to do with me than with them. I still carry the guilt of those events and the subsequent years. I am also constantly reminded how my pride and unwillingness to admit I didn't have the money or the answers made things much worse. Lastly, I am reminded every once in a while about that feeling I had that day as I walked out, how I looked around, but only barely. I had been given a warning, plain as day, and ignored it. Look at all of the heartaches and lost time that could have been avoided if I had just followed that instinct a little deeper into the debris on the workbench that day and found that ember before it was all gone.

Chapter 11

Everything Changes and Kids are Included but Batteries are Not.

December 1998 came faster than I wanted, and after a hell of a year, it was time to make some decisions. I was faced with deciding to renew the lease at the Paintball store for the arena. Business had been good, but the extra insurance and labor cost made it not worth it. I pulled the trigger and sold the rental fleet and support equipment to an operation in New Jersey on the beach. That left me to run a store closing/moving sale during the holiday rush, which was not reassuring to customers. The long year ended, and the actual net losses when you accounted for the past capital infusions were about two hundred thousand dollars. While I had taken a modest salary and pilfered double, I was still way short of making a case for it being a viable business. I had a few more tricks up my sleeves, but they were too late to make a lasting impact.

I had found a nice, smaller storefront close to the house that was perfect for the newly streamlined operations. I leveraged the existing inventory and the credit line I still had from the supplier and filled the store and a warehouse with the product. I sold everything for the right price, and for the first time since Splat City, I was operating a successful and reasonably profitable business. I also began to take out ads, listing very desirable gear combinations at extremely low prices. I would then count on the ability to either fulfill those orders quickly and cheaply or move the customer to a different product with higher margins.

It was managed from the store at first and eventually later right from the supplier, with them shipping from their location with my packing slip inside. I had discovered paintball drop shipping by accident, and it was an excellent business. But like all other things in my life at that time, all was not well. My interest in the company was waning, and something else had caught my eye.

Jill was a cute, ditsy blond with a fun disposition and great boobs. We had been dating casually for most of the summer and had gotten more serious once fall had rolled around. By the winter, we were inseparable. I would go days without even going to the paintball store. Instead, I would be hanging out with her, taking road trips, going out at night, pretending like I didn't have a care in the world. I'm sure that the redirection of my energy towards her had its roots in filling the void left by losing Darrell. This shift in attention also had to do with the fact I was turning eighteen and, in a relative sense, had the world by the balls. I had my own house, a stable of fancy cars, and had even managed to rub elbows with rockstars and elites on private jets.

By the spring of '99, my absence at the paintball store had started to cause real problems. I was so disinterested in things that when I couldn't get staff, I just wouldn't open. That, of course, had a very harmful effect on business, and within a few months, I counted on a single employee to keep everything afloat. It was about that time my supplier cut off my credit line. They cut it off not because I didn't pay the bill— I always paid it right before immediately running it back up again. More importantly, it was what I was using it for. I was buying the least profitable items for them. They couldn't make any money on the items I was buying because of how many I was buying. That large purchase volume was also limiting what was available for other stores.

On top of that, I was going direct to the manufacturer and buying more of the same items direct from them, leveraging the already low price I was getting from my supplier to drive down the manufacturer's price and vice versa. That circular pattern continued and was nearly one hundred percent fueled by their own credit line I just kept re-taping. Needless to say, that wasn't the kind of partner they wanted, and they cut me off.

If I had been in their shoes, I might have given a little more warning but ultimately taken the same approach. Cutting off the credit line was painful, but what happened next hurt even more. The supplier put a guy on a plane to come to my shop and take back their stuff. I'm sure they'd sent a letter and given me a few days' notice, but I'm also sure I ignored it or didn't bother opening it all. The deadline came and went, and they were not playing around; by the end of the week, their agent would be at the store to collect one way or another. They happened to send someone in on a day that I only had a casual employee working the store, so zero resistance was given. I was on one of my impromptu road trips with Jill, so I was several hours away in Nashville when I got the call. When I got back, the store was empty. They took everything, probably worth just over the fifty thousand I owed them.

But there was a complication—there's always a complication. A lot of what they took was actually a product from a manufacturer purchased on a separate credit line. Also of note, some of that product from the manufacturer was bought at a higher price than my supplier had offered. That inconsistency was doubly painful as I only got credit at National's cost, which was in some cases lower than what I had paid from the manufacturer. I did have money in the bank that could have fully covered one or the other credit lines, but not both. I paid off the manufacturer with the remaining cash and left the supplier to cover their balance out of the product they repossessed. By the end of the month, I had zero cash, zero product, and no suppliers willing to sell me products even if I had money. While I could have kept the whole absentee owner, leveraging one supplier to pay another, robbing Peter to pay Paul thing going for some time with perfect management and attention to detail, I didn't have either. Instead, through my hubris and poor management, I had put myself out of business in an instant instead of the years the old way would have.

The financial damage up to that point had been relatively low as far as mistakes like that went—until you considered the lease and a slowly growing pile of monthly payments and obligations that continued with or without a paintball store. The lease was terrible. In my rush to get an alternative to the arena cost, I agreed to an iron-clad lease that left me at the landlord's mercy, and they didn't have much mercy. Expenses like vehicles, phone book advertising, bills, and ongoing services were co-conspirators in the death of the arena, and absolutely guilty of killing American Paintball for good once I made the last few blunders. By that summer, I found myself in a curious place. Had I stayed in school like my peers, I would have been an eighteen-year-old high school graduate with the entire world in front of me. Instead, I found myself an eighteen-year-old high school drop-out with a GED and a string of suspect business experiences mixed with a healthy dose of dysfunction and a warped sense of success and entitlement. I lived like a millionaire, but that was now all over. I was at my lowest, just as everyone I knew was at their highest.

The final accounting of the money made and lost in the business over the years is tough to get right. It was used as a cash grab by Papaw and me to the tune of what must have been more than a million dollars over the years. It was also the recipient of about two hundred and fifty thousand dollars in cash over the same time. The business incurred debt, some paid and some that weren't. The total tally of gross receipts put the best year at well over a million dollars and the surrounding years between two and four hundred thousand dollars in volume, meaning it generated revenue. Whether it ever made real money that's a more complicated question. I suspect it did, but not in proper proportion to the amount of capital and manpower invested.

Is it a tricky question to answer when asked was it all worth it? Mathematically, NO—there were better places to place the money for future use. This short answer, while logical, does not consider whether the money was all going to be spent anyway. I contend that Papaw was heartbroken that he had lost Granny, and as a result, he did not plan on staying around much longer. That fatalist outlook led him to start to smoke again and generally live a very unhealthy lifestyle that would directly lead to his death years later. It would not be an unreasonable jump to say he didn't see the point in life after Granny died, and nearly all of his problems after the date of her death could, in one way or another, trace their origins to money. That desire to be rid of all things' money was compounded by my mother and aunt's jockeying for substantial payments and bailouts. They went as far as to use his grandsons as pawns, either through direct extortion like with me or by withholding contact like with my Aunt's child.

The money invested in the paintball store was not the end of his investments. He would also presumably purchase shares in a racehorse, a ladder company that manufactured step ladders, and a landscaping business. My only involvement was in the paintball store, and I suspect many of the others were scams, as nothing tended to materialize after the initial payments. In addition to the many frauds and promises of shares in the business, there were the gifts Papaw gave. Hundreds of thousands were given to anyone with a sob story and bad luck. I know of at least three cars and a second mortgage he paid off following a request for help. I know of several people my age that had at least a semester of college tuition paid for by him just because they asked and he was having a good day.

With this larger context established, I feel the proper way to ask if it was worth it is:

Do you regret taking the money from Papaw, the money you knew had no chance of being saved for a later date and future use as payment for your education instead? An education that covered diverse topics such as finance, psychology, and sociology while also giving you four years of executive-level lessons, including traveling the country, driving exotic cars to work, and living a life that would be enviable to the Instagram influencer's of today? Hell, yes, it was worth it, and Papaw knew that; and that is why he paid that bill first. I got a lot of experience and living for a relatively small amount of money. Would a perfectly invested and managed nest egg years later be nice to have, you bet. Would I trade them—**NO FUCKING WAY**.

To put this into a unique perspective, think about this. Four years of my son's college tuition with room and board cost about $200,000. If my son came to me with a business plan to open a paintball store costing the same amount instead of going to college, I would say where do you want me to sign. That is how firmly I believe in what Papaw did for me and how valuable I feel it was in making me the man I am today.

I do want to offer one caveat to the previous topic: the answers I am giving are based on my current adult perspective. This is a perspective I have shared most of the time since 1999. It is even a perspective I talked with Papaw about near the end of his life, so I am very confident. There was a time in the summer of 1999 I may have wavered a bit in my resolve. Things were not working out well, and I was undoubtedly a bit lost. It is safe to say my will returned within a few years, but it was tough. Here is a little more about those more challenging times, as they had as much impact on me as the easy ones.

Following the closing of the paintball store, I was suddenly liberated and trapped at the same time. I had a little cash left, but I needed that for the next part of my journey. I was free of burden and responsibility, but I was also without a safety net. I was l back living with Papaw and renting out my mom's old house for extra cash. I had decided I would reinvent myself and real estate was the best way to make that happen. My whole life, Papaw had either rehabbed houses for profit or in service of the family. I figured I could do the same thing. I had the tools and skills and some of the money I needed. I had a Realtor who would help me, and I was off. My first project was going to be easy. I inherited my Mom's old mobile home and the house in Burlington. The house still had a mortgage, but the mobile home was free and clear.

The problem with the mobile home was two-fold:

1. It had previously had a dead body sitting in it for a week in the August sun with no air conditioning.
2. It was too old to be allowed to stay in her mobile home park. I had heard they had made exceptions to the age rule in the past, but there were also complaints regarding disturbances—something about a Hummer and a mailbox. That didn't ring any bells, so I was stuck needing to move that hot tin can of death.

My Realtor had found me a vacant piece of land I would be able to move the trailer to. I would need to add a septic system and build a foundation. The water and electricity were already at the property. It was a nice two-acre lot on the top of a hill that was rather steep and featured two switchbacks. The deal was inked, and we dragged that thing onto the top of the mountain. That was when the problems started. The move had gone fine—the problem was with the bank. The cost of the property was fourteen thousand dollars. I had that money, no problem. I was also going to need another nine thousand dollars for improvements to the site—that I didn't have. The real estate venture was a solo thing for me, and Papaw couldn't help if he wanted to. He was tapped out, and his credit was terrible.

My credit wasn't good or bad; it just didn't exist. I went to my nearest local bank, where I had never done business, and started the process. I had too much pride and shame to go to a place that knew me; I was starting fresh. That bank could help, but there was a bit of miscommunication on the terms. They said they could help and give me a secured credit line for the purchase price of the land. Great, I would just use the cash in their bank to make the improvements, sell the place, pay back the balance of funds, and walk away happy. Then I got to the miscommunication part. They only wanted to extend the loan based on the cash security in the account and would reduce the available credit on the line as the cash balance decreased. They, of course, could provide this supremely useful service for about four thousand dollars in closing cost. That's right; they would only charge me four thousand dollars to loan me my own fourteen thousand dollars, still leaving me in need of another nine thousand dollars to complete the project. However, they would give me an excellent CD rate of about 0.6% on my deposit.

Thinking I must have gotten something wrong, I checked with no less than three different people, and I had understood these terms correctly. As it turned out, walking into a bank and borrowing money wasn't easy when you were eighteen if you didn't have a millionaire backing you and an existing relationship to lean on. Why hadn't someone told me this?

This and similar stories would repeat themselves over the next few months. I eventually got the project done through sheer grit and slow-paying vendors. I had learned some lessons from the paintball time and realized if you were slow to pay, that was OK if they knew you were going to be slow in the first place, and you paid handsomely for the privilege. I rolled into my next project with a slightly larger bankroll, and this time tried my luck at getting an actual mortgage. Somehow, I got past both the credit and lack of income verification as it was the early 2000s. I, however, got stuck on the repairs that were needed at the property. They could only do the loan if the property were in good shape, but I couldn't have bought it if it was in good condition. I negotiated a sweet deal with the help of my Realtor. I would repair the house using my own funds prior to the close, and as long as the repairs were complete prior to the closing, my mortgage would close. That approach was pretty high stakes because if I got ninety percent of the way but didn't finish the repairs, my loan wouldn't close, but I also wouldn't get back my money used for repairs. Taking the project to the literal wire, it finally closed, but with a tiny hiccup.

To close the loan, they needed to see six months of reserves in the bank. No one had told me this beforehand, and I had used all my reserves and then some to get the place done. I had to turn to Papaw to bail me out. He then turned to his brother to bail both of us out. This was the last time Papaw bailed me out with money, and I was always grateful to both him and his brother as I would have been sunk before I started without that money. That house sold, but it took a few months. By the time the books were squared, I had a nice little profit.

I also had a nice little bun in the oven. That's right, on one of our weekend trips, that time to Gatlinburg, Jill got pregnant. This news was going to complicate things; I just didn't know by how much. I have talked about expectations and their power over my life a few times. Whether they were expectations from others or ones I placed on myself, they were—and sometimes still are—a very real part of my life. In the case of being a parent and potentially a spouse, I felt my life had been lacking as a child, and I was determined to make up for that. I was going to give my child the best and most elaborate environment possible. I made it my goal to provide everything for my spouse and be the best husband and dad. Those were all the expectations I had placed on myself.

Jill, unfortunately, had a similar version of what both of those roles would look like. I'm sure she compromised on some aspects, but she was going to shoot for the moon as I certainly wasn't telling her no. These lofty goals ended up becoming her expectations. I'll give you a second to guess how my own and her expectations played out... About as you would expect. We very quickly moved in together and played house. I spent money I didn't have making improvements to the house and built an entirely separate apartment for us, complete with a kitchen, bathroom, and separate entrance. The idea was we could still be around to look after Papaw but have our own place.

Within a few months, I found myself unable to meet the impossible expectations I had set for myself. By the eighth month, I had wholly failed to meet Jill's less impossible expectations, and she moved back home with her mom. That choice wasn't entirely Jill's as she was under some pressure from her mother, but I certainly made it easy for her. By that time, the reality was also setting in, and I would have to give up the real estate business as I had run out of capital in an endless pursuit of something that could not be caught. Hailey Katheryn White was born in August of 2000. She was beautiful and amazing, but there was a new problem—having just seen how perfect she was, I was even more confident I could never let her down. I needed a whole new set of even loftier expectations and standards I could hold myself to in order to be worthy of her perfectness.

A few months after she was born, Jill and I got an apartment together. I had been working on finding a job and was having lots of luck getting them, just not as much luck convincing myself I needed to keep them. The pattern was always the same: I would easily get the job under the guise of some management training program, etc. I would work for about three weeks, stocking shelves and maybe counting down the cash register at night. I would receive my first check and instantly be reminded I wasn't the boss anymore. Not only was I not the boss, but I was also almost certainly making things worse by even working. I told myself I would have been better off taking the last $300- to $400 we had left and buying some funny t-shirts or getting bumper stickers printed to sell at the flea market. Heck, I could buy a beat-up lawn mower and make more than that cutting grass. I wasn't wrong, but Jill and her family didn't want me hustling; they wanted me working. If I would just shut up and keep my head down one day, I might be able to be the assistant manager. If we were really lucky, we would be able to use a credit card to take a trip to Disney World once. It's funny how expectations work—even if they are not exceptionally high, they can still be tough to reach. I was falling short of my expectations for myself—daily, I could live with that. The bigger problem was I was falling short of Jill's expectations—and ultimately her family's—and they were meager expectations. Falling short of those expectations was harder to live with because I already knew the consequences.

Within six months, Jill and I had broken up. We would try a few more times to make it work, but we never could quite figure it out. We were both incredibly supportive of each other and shared a love for many years, but we were never officially together after that. Jill enrolled in college by the end of the year and regularly attended, working on a communications degree. On top of receiving her education, she also figured out how to make the excess grant funds and student loans last until the following semester. She would combine that money with her tax returns and what little I was able to give her. As it turned out, Jill had been paying attention and watching me as I hustled, and she had turned into quite the little hustler herself. Jill ended up in a new apartment in the same complex as the one I had helped move Papaw into a few months before.

Papaw could no longer afford the house with just his social security money, and I couldn't help him with much, so he ended up in a value-priced, one-bedroom apartment. I would spend the night on his couch when I didn't have anywhere else to go—which was often. After I broke up with Jill, I didn't have an actual full-time place I could call my own. I wasn't homeless, but I certainly didn't have a permanent address to call my own. When I had enough money for a bar tab, I was known to try my luck with the ladies. My selectiveness was generally correlated with my desire to not sleep on my Papaw's couch that night.

We have all heard of hobos—well, I was basically a hobosexual, ostensibly homeless, but for not having the opportunity to share an evening with a beautiful, young host. I wasn't working a consistent real job much at that time. I would deliver pizza in the evenings to get free food and some walking around money. During the day, I would hustle, doing just about anything someone would pay me for. One week it was building a deck; the next, it might be cleaning out an old hoarder's house. It was never enough money to get ahead, but it was enough to get by. I would give Jill some and live off what was left while sharing with Papaw when I could.

Papaw and I had developed a system to help each other out that wasn't all that different from the paintball cash register. We would ask each other how much the other had, and we could take up to half of what the other had without question. That took some discipline and maturity, but it was a way for us to make the change in our circumstances work. We never could abuse the system because the other would do the same thing back the next day. You didn't ask if you didn't need it, and if they asked, you gave, even if you needed it.

By that time, the whole college thing looked like a viable option. It would allow me to have a consistent place to live and possibly give me a path forward. I wasn't optimistic, but I let Jill give me a few pointers, and thanks to the GED my Mom made me get, I was able to enroll. I didn't have transcripts or verifiable work history, which meant I couldn't go in as a normal student. Still, the University of Cincinnati had a program for nontraditional students that allowed you to live on campus in a dorm and attend basic 099 level classes—kind of like college with training wheels. Part of the enrollment in that program included applying for and receiving federal aid such as housing and meals you qualified for. As I filled out my form, it became clear that I was eligible for food assistance or food stamps. It was easy to qualify as I was an orphan with my Mom dead and my Dad dead to me.

At that point, I had essentially come full circle in my life. When I was born, I was on food stamps, as my memories of that roach-infested apartment included boxes of government cheese and generically-labeled food. Later in life, I was privileged and benefited from the stability afforded by a family with resources. By the time I was seventeen, I had lived a millionaire's lifestyle with cars, houses, trips, and enough cash to choke a horse. I don't know whether or not I ever had a million dollars in cash in my hands at once, but indeed there were many weeks and months in which I was a fractional millionaire. Three short years later, I found myself right back where I started—on food stamps and trying to live up to expectations, but this time instead of just being the expectations others placed on me, I had a few of my own to add along with them.

I started the fall semester in 2001 at twenty-one years old. At that point in my life, I had both been on food stamps and a millionaire, and now I was back on food stamps again. Something tells me I was doing things in the wrong order.

Chapter 12

Marriage, My First Career, and Hints of What's to Come

As the fall of 2001 started, I was quickly acclimating to my new dorm room. Don't confuse acclimating with enjoying because they are two very different things. I suppose a prisoner eventually acclimates to his cell but probably never fully enjoys that same cell. That was school for me—at least the living on campus part. I had fully expected a period of adjustment, I had been an outside cat my whole life, and now I was being forced into a situation that was decidedly not free-range. For perhaps the first time since living in old Burlington, I found myself subject to the rules and restrictions that dictated when and where I could or couldn't go. This circumstance was intentional on my part. I had anticipated my possible discontent with school and figured the surest way to guarantee success was to make certain school was the only thing I had. I would eat, sleep, and breathe school for the next several years and come out the other side as a doctor. That was my plan, at least.

A few days before classes started was move-in day for the dorms. The campus was busy and full of families and teens taking their first steps as adults. It's safe to say my experience had little in common with theirs. The day's first task was getting my room assignment, Dabney Hall. That dorm was probably one of the oldest on campus but was considered to be relatively quiet as it housed other adult students. My dorm was a small concrete block cell—I mean room—with a series of built-in wooden closets/wardrobes on one side. It was in good repair, clean, and just received a fresh coat of calming, institutional-green paint. My cell was on the fourth floor and looked out towards Shoemaker Center. I knew assault charges would be hard to get out of, so I spared everyone the hassle and chose the single room versus having a roommate. However, since I had a single room, I didn't have a private bathroom, which meant my designated showers and toilets were at the end of the hall. I didn't have much stuff—which was good because I didn't need much. I had bought a set of school clothes using the $300 left from my first student loans, along with a few necessities like a backpack and other basics. I hadn't worked out what I was planning on doing about books or even a laptop at that point. On the subject of loose ends, I had also neglected to figure out the parking situation, which would be an issue almost immediately. I had bought the meal plan that included three meals a day from the dining hall in the building next door.

Fairly quickly, I settled into a routine. I went to my classes—which were all in a single building—and joined twenty to thirty other teenagers for 099 courses. While I was only two years older than most other students, the age difference was shocking and instantly hit me. At twenty, I already had a child, owned and lost a business, and dealt with the shit show that was my life up until that point. Compare my experience to other students whose most extensive adversity up until then was losing a high school football game or not being asked to prom. As I mentioned, the classes were of the 099 variety. If you're not familiar with these, are the classes colleges make you take before you can have actual college classes. You have to pay for them and do all the work, but they don't count towards graduation or anything else. These remedial classes are also very controlled, requiring perfect attendance and participation. Since I hadn't had any ACT scores or transcripts from high school, that is just what they gave me. I excelled in all of the classes, except writing, in which I still earned a solid grade. The writing class was challenging, not because I couldn't write, but because the prompts were so mind-numbingly one-dimensional. These limited prompts were further burdened by the grading done by the other students, who were as equally obtuse. After the first midterms, I started to formulate some opinions about school. Combine these insights with my triggered intuition, and I knew something was up.

I found it odd that all of my classes were in a single building when nearly everyone I talked to complained about walking across campus for their classes. I also found it odd that a lot of attention was being placed on proper study skills like getting plenty of sleep and having a light at your desk. These skills, while helpful, should have probably already existed for a college student. The last hint something was off was when you took an objective view of the racial makeup of both my dorm and my classes. In any one dorm building or classroom, one would expect that the makeup of races among that group would generally match that of the general student population. In the case of Dabney Hall and the classes held in the University Center building, that hypothesis was dead wrong and could even be taken a little further. Nearly all students in my classes came from a specific geographic area, comprised mostly of poor, urban youth with traditionally under performing schools.

By the end of that first semester, I had put everything together and figured it out. The "adult student" was code for "didn't or couldn't graduate from high school." I had confused this term with "mature or nontraditional student," which meant coming back or just starting college after having time in the workforce as an adult. The entire "University College" and community-based housing policy was a scam. It operated almost like a social service or aid program. It was some sort of extension of high school that allowed people to feel like they were going to college and getting to live in the dorms because they didn't have anywhere else to go. Understanding this also explained why somehow the rules and security at my dorm seemed stronger than in other dorms. To get into Dabney, you had to go through an ID check every time, regardless of if you had a key. If you had a guest, they had to complete a sign-in and out. In all the other dorms, you simply got on an elevator. There might have been someone at a desk, but they merely took the fact you had a key to the building or a student ID on a lanyard as proof enough you belonged there. Those discrepancies extended to rules about quiet hours as well. In my dorm, they actively monitored the halls for people walking around or sitting in communal areas after a specific time, like parents checking curfew. In the other halls, quiet hours meant you had to party inside your room, not outside, but you were still free to congregate and socialize as long as you were respectful.

Once discovering that I was in some sort of kinder college with watchful parents and arbitrary rules, I resolved to make some changes. I met with my advisor, and despite his strongest objections, I signed up for real classes the following semester. I also managed to get out of my housing contract early and received a refund for the unused portion of the funds. I couldn't get a refund on the meal plan as I technically could still eat on campus while I had classes. Their approach seemed to make no allowance for the fact I would be living off-campus and would need to make special trips back to campus just to eat the meals I had already paid for. I needed a new place to stay, and I still very much wanted it to be integrated into the college experience. With midyear housing options limited, I settled on an odd choice. I was going to join a fraternity. I know—what you were thinking—but this particular house was not the stereotypical frat. Yes, we had a few parties, but it was more of a housing corporation with some social structure. The rent and dues were still less than an apartment's rent. Along with a room, I got Internet, stolen cable, and parking, which was a plus as I had been playing a cat and mouse game of hiding the cheese with parking enforcement since arriving on campus. From an age perspective, they we all older, like me as freshmen usually were not allowed to live in the house. Culturally, it was a bit of a juxtaposing situation when it came to Hailey. We would hang out in and around the house and campus during the day, and in the evenings, go back to Jill's house, where I would watch her there while Jill went out with her friends. That certainly wasn't an ideal situation, but it was what I had, and it only had to work until the end of the school year.

I finished that school year with honors in both my fake and real classes. The fraternity was happy as my grades improved the house average and got the fraternity off academic probation. I didn't sign up for summer classes in 2002 as I would focus on hustling and getting something restarted with my real estate dreams. I continued delivering pizzas at night and on the weekends and hustling daily. That all came crashing to a sudden stop on Memorial Day weekend of 2002—literally.

I was delivering pizzas just before the holiday when another driver in an intersection t-boned me. I can still picture it happening. He was coming from my left, driving a blue Cutlass or Monte Carlo, and I noticed he was going pretty fast and didn't show any signs of stopping. It happened as I got to the intersection with a steady green light. I can hear the sound of that shitty American car revving at full speed as it hits me on the driver's door. My ears rang from both the initial sound of the impact and the airbags hitting me. I remember my arms burning, first from the airbag and then as we came to rest from the hot coolant sprayed on me from the other car. The impact was violent and devastating. It wasn't just one hit, but several. The first was his car hitting mine, then my car bouncing off a pole and landing in a ditch, and then the last hit for good measure from his car coming to rest against mine.

I had always been good about wearing my seatbelt, but that day I was in a hurry and hadn't put it on between stops. In a miracle of circumstances, that lack of attention saved my life. As his car hit mine, I was thrown away from the door with my right leg stuck in the foot well. I floated in space, tethered by my leg as the airbags went off and the second impact of the pole happened. That second impact twisted the car and threw me to the passenger floor of my car. When his car stopped, it was almost right back where it first impacted with the bumper—or what was left of the bumper—sitting at the mid line of the driver's seat.

I was pinned in the car, stunned and ears ringing. I can distinctly remember the voices and sounds of the bystanders. One was an off-duty paramedic, and he was asking for Air Care. There was a woman who said she was a nurse helping me. She had blond hair and tan skin and wore a teal or aqua shirt with light-colored shorts. She tried to make sure I was OK, and I just told her to watch out for the glass. The accident happened just a mile from a full-time firehouse, so crews were on the scene fast. Out of the corner of my eye, I could see my phone lying just within reach on the floor. It was one of the old bulletproof Nokia models with rubber buttons and a green screen. I called the pizza place and told them I was in a wreck, and they would need to remake so-and-so's order. The firefighters had to cut me out of the car to free my leg. They loaded me in the same ambulance as the other driver, who was fine—very drunk, but fine.

As it turned out, the Air Care was for me, but through some miracle, I didn't need it. The only person I had to call was Papaw or Jill. I called Jill and told her what happened, and I wouldn't be able to take Hailey that weekend after all, and told her to call Papaw. Instead of calling him, she went down to his apartment and picked him up. They arrived at the hospital shortly after I did. They were followed by my manager, Chris, with who I had become good friends from the previous years of working together. He was my new Scott, as we routinely patrolled the bars and clubs, me as a college kid and him as a thirty-something gay man with a country accent; I'm sure it was quite the sight.

When he saw me, he started to cry as he had driven by the scene and saw them still investigating and cleaning up—apparently; it was pretty bad. In the end, I escaped with only a broken leg. It was a pretty nasty fracture at the tib-fib connection on the bottom of my knee that would eventually require a total, open reduction and many screws, plates, and even a little cadaver bone to patch up. Surgery was scheduled for a few days later, and I would be one hundred percent off my feet for at least six weeks.

I spent the first two days after surgery at the hospital, having scammed the second day by saying I didn't have anyone to help at home. That wasn't true, as it was summer and the frat house was deserted. Further disqualifying the frat house was a lack of an actual bathtub and three flights of stairs, both of which were no Buenos. After being released, I recovered on a series of couches and recliners. A little at Chris's, some at Papaw's, and even a little at Jill's. The doctors said six weeks, so I took that as a challenge to do it in three, which was not long enough. Since I was hardheaded, I had a fall and got an infection that turned the original six weeks into about ten total. There isn't much else to say about the wreck or its outcome. I was fortunate—as in only through the grace of god lucky—to have survived that day. When it was over, I carried the weight of that with me in many ways. I had even told Jill we should get married and explained she and Hailey were the first things I thought about after the wreck. It was a sweet jester on my part, and we entertained the idea for about three days, but in the end, we were both on different journeys.

That summer, I learned to be thankful and to have a greater appreciation for the few friends and resources I did have. If it weren't for Chris, I wouldn't have been able to get by as he served as my taxi service and companion the whole time I was confined to that wheelchair. That wouldn't be the last thing I had to thank Chris for, but I'll tell you about him helping me meet my wife a little later.

The fall of 2002 had me back at school and living at the frat house again. I had switched my classes to remote and evening, not knowing if mobility and getting around would be a problem. I had also begun to develop a sense of urgency related to school. I don't know if it was the crash or being twenty-one with a kid and living in a frat house. By then, I had also set any aspirations of a medical career aside. Instead, I focused on what could get me out of school the quickest and easiest. I switched my field to construction and was planning on first finishing my associates and later my bachelor's while I was working in the field. One additional benefit of this change was that I could co-op for myself. That meant while I was doing my thing and hustling, I could also get school credit for it. After the wreck, I found a client that needed my construction expertise and energy to assist in the rehab of a large, historic building. The client had agreed in exchange for me managing the planning and pre-construction phases to allow me to stay in an apartment they owned nearby. That was a match made in heaven. I finally had an actual place of my own and was able to be useful to someone.

All I had to do was find suitable design professionals who could help deliver a completed design and preservation package that allowed the project to move forward. Lucky for me, I knew exactly where to look for those design pros—school. They were my professors and teachers; all I had to do was talk them into helping, and everybody would be happy. They would make some extra money, I got an apartment and college credit, and my partner got the design package completed for a relative bargain—everybody wins. That plan was great in theory. I found a professor that could do the work and made the introductions. He received a small advance and was on his way. I was putting in the footwork of detailing every nook and cranny of the building. I spent my days taking detailed measurements and making drawings of each piece of trim and gingerbread in the hope of deciding if it stayed or went. One week turned into two and two weeks into months, and my client was starting to get nervous—as was I.

We still hadn't received any of the promised drawings from the professor. In my mind, I had already guessed where this was heading and started to formulate a plan. The professor had run off with the money and went on a bender. The very few drawings he had sent me were incomplete, with only twenty percent being usable. Luckily for me, I had paid attention in class and went to work. I just did the drawings myself. They were my first set of architectural drawings, and they were terrible. My drawings provided some of the needed details but lacked many others. The drawings would have to be redone before the project started, but they were good enough for now. They got the project past the initial concept phase and into the actual design and estimating phase. For the amount of money my client paid, the drawings were grossly under-delivered and were not a fair value. However, considering the inferior quality of what I had to work with and the fact I was only paid in trade with a few months' rent for an apartment on the second floor of a lesbian karaoke club, it was a win for everyone.

That experience would be the beginning of the end of school for me. That situation actually repeated itself with another professor later that year, and I was done. I wasn't going to pay tuition with the money I didn't have, only to be taught by people without integrity and, many times, even the most basic skills. They were costing me money and two fronts, which wasn't working for me. There was another factor at play; I had managed to find an investor willing to risk financing rehab houses with me in exchange for a splitting of the profits. That, of course, was as long as I was willing/able to find the properties, do all of the repair work, maintain the properties before the sale, and absorb any carrying cost out of my half of the profits. Beggars can't be choosers, and it sure beats having to fire your professors and listing to lesbian karaoke while trying to sleep.

By the summer of '03, I had started to eke out a living with my new partners. We had done one deal already, and I had walked away with about $20,000 for a few months of work. I paid many bills and bought a used truck while repeating the process. That new endeavor had another unintended benefit—it gave me a place to stay. It was usually a shitty place to stay, but it was a place. Once we bought a new house, I would move in, sometimes even living in a tent inside the home if the condition was bad enough. I would make it a priority to fix a bathroom and heat right away. I would then move outward from there until I had a comfortable place. I could justify this because my presence provided security, and I shouldered any additional cost from a lack of progress out of my half of the profits. With this new setup, I had gone from hobosexual to dorm, to frat house, to lesbian Karaoke apartment, to now being a vagrant living in abandoned houses. I was moving up in the world.

The downside with this approach was I never really had furniture. I lived out of a single closet where I would put a locking doorknob. Each morning, I would pack it away in case of showings. My air mattress, clothes, and shaving kit were all neatly stored in the closet, hidden from view. I would snack for breakfast, eat out for lunch, and at that point, usually drank my dinner, so I didn't have much need for a kitchen. My life wasn't great at that point, but it was workable. I was building up a little money—or certainly wasn't going backward. I was free. I was able to help Papaw out and pay Jill child support. The biggest thing I missed was being able to spend time with Hailey, doing nothing. Because of my living situation, every time Hailey and I did something together; it always had to be something—go to a museum, a park, Totter Otterville, visit Papaw, something. We could never just lay on a couch, watching a movie, or hang out with nothing particular planned. When I had the karaoke apartment, she had a small play area/room painted pink that was just hers, but that wasn't enough. That feeling of needing to not live like a hobo was starting to accumulate in my mind, and I would be waiting for the right moment to make itself known.

That lifestyle was not all bad. I was young and generally had an appetite for having a good time. I had a few friends, like Chris and Libby, who were single and knew by heart the schedule of every local pub's promotion—$5 buckets, $2 Tuesday, and college night for three counties. There was always something to do or people to see, and if I was hungover the following day, I could always just tell the boss I wanted to start an hour later. I was never a particularly hard drinker as I had always avoided it growing up. Before my twenty-first birthday, I had approximately three full beers and had gotten drunk on one occasion off bourbon. To this day, I can't drink bourbon because of that night. While I was not typically a heavy drinker, at twenty-two, everything you do seems to revolve around alcohol in one way or another. That hot summer night at Barrett's Sports Bar was no exception. Chris had convinced me to go with him, and I can never repay him for making it possible for me to meet the hard-partying, heavy drinking, woman of my dreams named Allison.

I had perfected my persona at that point. I was a young real estate investor and bachelor; I even had business cards to prove it if someone didn't believe me (for real estate, not being a bachelor). I would usually start a conversation and offer to buy them a drink. Back in my hobo days, I had developed a twist to this move that I have since trademarked. The twist involved purchasing a drink for both the girl and her inevitable friend. One in ten would then have you buy a drink for their boyfriend or date, which was bad, but "them's the breaks." Three out of ten would politely decline and either try to engage in small talk or say they were about to leave, but the next six out of ten would gladly accept. Here is the special part—that's not six girls, but rather twelve potentials. Using the double approach, I could hit twenty girls in ten attempts and only buy fourteen drinks at most. Of the fourteen drinks, twelve would be actual possibilities—that's a sixty percent success rate. I'll take those odds. Who said math didn't have real-world applications?

The logic was if a girl were on the fence, she would have her friend saying to her, "Hey, that was nice of him to buy us both drinks." If the primary target was otherwise unavailable, her friend didn't feel shunned or like a second-class option. That night at Barret's, I was feeling saucy—no doubt excited that I had just fixed the air conditioner in the house I was working on and would be able to sleep on my blowup mattress without sweating my ass off. I came up to a table of six girls. They were all reasonably attractive and pleasant. They looked to be out on a girl's night out—which in my experience, was almost as good as a bachelorette party or Valentine's Day. I made small talk for a few minutes, and then I did it; I pulled my move. "I would like to buy a drink for everyone at the table; what would you guys like to drink?" At first, they probably thought I was a waiter or something, but then it clicked. It had worked. They were super impressed and began ordering their drinks one by one. First was a long island, then a piña colada, a couple of margaritas, and a mimosa. The last girl looked me square in the eyes and said, "If you're going to spend the money, I want a pitcher of beer." Despite the disapproving looks from her friends, she stood her ground and said make it Bud Light.

I went back up to the bar and grabbed each drink, bringing them back to the table. When I got the pitcher back, I asked if she wanted one cup or if she was going to share it with me, to which she responded in a pleasant but firm tone, "Get your own; this is mine." My multiple-girl gamble had worked, and I talked to people from the group all night. By the end of the evening, I had found out they made this night and location a regular thing. While I talked to a few girls, I spent the most time talking to a cute girl named Jamie. She was the one who had ordered the long island. We exchanged numbers, and she invited me to meet her and her friends at the same place the following week. Having since graduated from being a hobo, I took the number as a win and closed out my night. I talked to Jamie a few times during the week, and we were hitting it off—nothing too serious, but overall, I was hopeful. The following Tuesday rolled around, and I met the whole crew again at Barrettes. There were even a few fresh faces this time.

I have to say the vibe was a little off from how I expected it to be. Everyone was friendly, but Jamie was extra distant. We managed to talk a little around the group, and then she asked to speak to me privately. That wasn't good. I didn't know what to expect, but I knew it wouldn't be good. As it turned out, Jamie had a boyfriend—which on its own wouldn't be a problem—but the fact he was also coming to Barrett's was. We agreed to no harm, no foul, and I wouldn't mention it again. As we were wrapping up, she said, "Hey, why don't you try talking to Allison? She thought you were cute last week." I agreed, never to turn down a referral, but I didn't know which one was Allison.

We walked into the larger room with the dance floor, and she reintroduced me to Allison, the girl who had ordered the whole pitcher of beer and wouldn't share it. Allison quickly made eye contact and looked me up and down. She was literally sizing me up. I didn't know if she was going to grade me or fight me. She asked if I wanted to buy her another pitcher of beer and motioned toward the bar with her eyes. That time she shared the pitcher with me, and we hung out all night. At the night's end, we were milling about the parking lot, watching the shit show of drunk people getting into cars with random strangers and taxi cabs pulling away with their unconscious cargo. The night was over, and she handed me a tiny, rolled-up piece of paper with her home phone number and said, "You better call me." I got a small kiss before she walked over to her friends.

That was the second week in a row that I was leaving the bar without company, but somehow, I knew this would be different. Over the next few days, we talked a ton. She didn't have a cell phone, so I would call her Mom's house and ask to speak with her, it was very awkward but also sweet. At first, she was skeptical about me, my job, and especially Hailey, and how that would all work out. By our fourth date, I told her I loved her, and she was saying it back by the next. The first time I spent the night with her at her Mom's house we didn't even make out, instead we filled the evening talking about music. She hadn't invited me over to make out, instead, she wanted to show me her CD collection and talk about what music was essential to her. I left that night with an intense desire to make love to her, and a stack of CDs containing the soundtrack to her life.

Allison got pregnant on New Year's 2004. We had been together for five or six months living between whatever shit hole I was working on and her childhood room at her mom's house. Allison had been engaged once before and very nearly got married. She had gone as far as to have already bought the wedding dress for that wedding. That hadn't worked out the previous spring, and she had moved back home, heartbroken and lost. That circumstance—and perhaps partially that empty place in her heart—landed her out with her friends that summer night when we met. I was happy to fill the empty spot for her. Once we found out she was pregnant, we talked about marriage. We both approached it matter-of-factually and agreed we would be okay with marrying each other. Initially, there was no proposal or big moment of "YES" but rather a quite acknowledgment that, yeah, we were both good with this. It might have been a little sooner than either of us had anticipated, but I think by that point, we both viewed us getting married as an inevitability, even before she was pregnant.

We planned a quick wedding at the Justice of the Peace but were hampered by a lack of witnesses. We had planned on going back later that day with the fifty dollars required to pay for a homeless fellow to witness our joyous event. During that intermission, we told Allison's Mom of our plans. Her Mom—a devote Irish catholic—would have nothing of the sort. An alternative demand was made in what would be a familiar pattern of "how could you do this to me" and "what will everyone think." We would get married in the church, and it would happen quickly. Valentine's Day was only a few weeks away, so Allison's Mom decided—or more accurately, issued as a decree—that we would be married at her Mom's childhood church on Valentine's Day 2004.

Allison wore the dress she already had, and I wore a tuxedo rented for me by my future brother-in-law. She was stunning that day. Her bouquet was of a particular flair as it included the tattered remnants of her most precious childhood toy, "Bunny." Allison made an honest man of me that day in front of our friends and family. The reception was held at a hall donated to us by my business partner. It was a decidedly do-it-yourself affair, with Allison and me handling the printing of the invitations and the creation of the centerpieces. Allison managed the playlist herself, and her parents dealt with the food, drinks, and flowers. The mother of her childhood friend provided the cake, and her Uncle printed the programs.

Overall, it was a beautiful event. Much like a funeral, it probably meant a lot more for the people attending than it did for the people at the center of attention. The days and weeks leading up to the wedding weren't without some controversy. Allison was struggling to have her desires heard over her mom's wishes. There were issues involving jealousy that kept Hailey from getting to participate as a flower girl. Even a bit of a scandal related to my Dad's Mom (my Grandma) not being mentioned in the program at the reception. This omission was unintentional as I didn't make the programs, but unfortunately, it would have a lasting effect. We had a short honeymoon at the Sheraton Hotel in Norwood, Ohio, following the wedding. We arrived at about 11 p.m. and were greeted with an air conditioner that wouldn't turn off. We spent precisely seven hours in the suite before being abruptly evicted by the cleaning crew; they were in a hurry to make the room up for the next guest arriving that day. Hopefully, their honeymoon was longer than ours.

Chapter 13

Life Keeps Being Hard but a Career Helps

Following our wedding in 2004, Allison and I started to make a life for ourselves. We stayed at her mom's house at that time as the newest rehab project wasn't going well. More correctly, the project was going fine when I worked on it. The issue was with everything else, the pregnancy, marriage, and the honeymoon, I had lost focus. Once the project was done, that additional delay from a lack of focus caused an issue related to my partner being slow to release the funds from the project. It was, in my mind, a simple issue, as I was already being penalized for the extra delay on my profit. I couldn't help but feel that my partner viewed my new marriage as causing a deeper problem; maybe I wasn't going to be the workaholic rehab machine I once was, and maybe without that extra oomph, I was just another contractor not worthy of the additional risk or investment. Either way, the funds I needed for my new family were delayed, causing tension. The funds would eventually get released, but it happened in two batches across months. The distrust and frustration were growing on both sides.

Keller was born that summer, which meant that it was time to make some decisions. Allison and I rented our first apartment together, a charming Italianate first-floor unit with hardwood floors and beautiful, tall windows. There was wide trim and character galore. That beautiful apartment would usually be out of our price range, but it was also about half a block from the ghetto. It had zero off-street parking and was whore-house adjacent. Our business arrangement was at an impasse by the fall, and we walked away from the last project. Because we walked away, it meant there would be no compensation for the work done, but we were OK with that. We still had our tools and each other. Shortly after we decided to walk away from the last project, most of our tools were stolen while being stored in a secure shop. That shop was only accessible by us, our previous partner, and the new crew who replaced us on the last project. While everybody denies responsibility, it's safe to say that event was the end of both a partnership and a relationship.

I took a job with a local construction company that fall as a project manager and quickly found myself with the first job I didn't hate. I was treated well and respected. They expected a lot out of me, and in return, I gave them my full effort. Allison had gone back to work teaching at a daycare. While not her favorite job, it came with the benefit of including childcare which was a critical help for us. Times for us were tough. I can distinctly remember one week paying our bills and writing a 37¢ check to someone. That wasn't the amount we owed; it was just the amount we had left and could afford to send. We had our drives to work counted out by the mile with gas calculated to the penny and not a single diversion or detour to spare. Trying to save money, we had bought a small food processor to make Keller's baby food from scratch as it was way cheaper to buy a pound of green beans versus 20 jars of baby food. Allison and I ate pureed vegetables with every meal for the next several weeks as Keller much preferred the taste of jarred baby food.

Speaking of Keller, it is important to note that he wasn't doing great. It wasn't anything specific but more generalities. He was a very fussy baby—not just by our standards but even by the standards of the daycare workers and others that held him. He would cry, and that cry was quite fierce. The crying would go for hours and only stop with his exhaustion. The pediatricians suggested different formulas, eventually landing on one that helped a little, but there was a problem—that formula was almost eighty dollars a can. Each can would last a little less than a week. That was a tall burden for new parents counting pennies to cover our expenses. Having had some experience with babies, I noticed other peculiarities, Keller didn't seem to respond to his name or speech the way Hailey had. He did not respond to lullabies or singing. The only thing that would help him was to have his bare body against yours and gently pat him. Over the next several months, we had as many as ten more visits to the pediatrician, each ending in a frustrating "well, some babies are just fussy" by the doctors. On a few occasions, they would say he had an earache and prescribe some drops, but nothing serious or of consequence. Allison had been withstanding the worst of Keller's issues that year as she was often the one left comforting him at 4 a.m. Allison also took the feeling of helplessness the hardest. While we both felt something was wrong, Allison was his mother and thought she should have been able to fix the situation.

By the spring of 2005, the newness of being married and having a child had worn away. We loved how our apartment looked, but after my car was stolen the same week, we watched a mob of kids beat a twelve-year-old girl in the street and knew it was time to go. Luckily, we found a new place closer to Allison's mom for about the same price. Our landlords seemed to acknowledge the neighborhood's shortcomings and agreed to let us leave a few months early without penalty. The new apartment wasn't as pretty, but it was safe. Allison had also started to find her voice and independence around that time. I don't know if it was the walks from the car to the house each night or just being fed up with not being able to help Keller, but she grew some balls and confronted our pediatrician. She demanded Keller be given a referral to a specialist, to which the doctor replied, "Before we can do that, we have to document a series of infections." Allison quickly retorted, "What do you think the last six months have been?" The doctor offered one last half-hearted explanation about it just being one infection, blah, blah, but Allison wouldn't give up. Allison left the office that day with a referral to see a specialist at Children's Hospital. Her instincts as a mother wouldn't let her leave the office without it. It took a few weeks to get all the proper medical records sent over and make the appointment. When we finally got to see a specialist, it didn't take long to get some answers.

Keller had been suffering from a persistent infection in both ears that was resistant to antibiotics. That infection had begun to dissolve the tiny bones in his ear and was causing permanent damage. He was in constant pain from the ear infections; he was unable to hear all but the loudest stimuli. That explained the fervent crying and that he could only be soothed by touch. That also explained his lack of reaction to our voices and the odd pronating and disorientation he exhibited anytime you held him. For nearly a year, that baby had suffered from an earache and vertigo without ever hearing the comfort of his parent's voices. No wonder he was so hard to soothe. Allison, of course, blamed herself as any mother would, but it wasn't her fault. It was the fault of the arrogant and bureaucratic pediatricians that would rather see one or two extra patients in a day than spend actual substantive time with a parent to hear what they are saying. Keller received two rounds of strong IV antibiotics and had drain tubes placed soon after. That would be the first of many surgeries for Keller, but at least it was a start. Following the treatments and tubes, he slowly improved. Keller was quickly becoming like any other boy his age; as his recovery progressed, a huge weight was lifted off of our shoulders.

Keller's hearing wasn't the only new thing that summer; I was about to start an adventure that would span the next seventeen years. The journey would take our young family on the adventure of a lifetime and allow us to see an experience that no one would have thought possible—and it all started with a tiny, classified ad in the paper.

Help Wanted: Construction Estimator

Assist with storm recovery by measuring and documenting damage

Travel required

Start Immediately

Ask for Charlie

I called the number listed and spoke with Charlie for a few minutes. It was agreed on the call that I would come down for a formal interview the next day. That worked out as I was working on a project close to his office, and I could interview during my lunch break. I'm not sure what even made me look at the paper in the first place; it wasn't something I did with any regularity. I was happy with my current job as it was paying OK and provided a good opportunity in its own right.

It's hard to explain, but something about that opportunity just called me—like it was magnetic, drawing my attention to it. Like a few other occasions in my life, that moment had a certain buzz or instinct about it. I arrived right on time for my interview, which lasted about an hour. We switched between formal, technical questions and discussions to more free-flowing topics. We got along well, and I had a good understanding of the job by the end. I was to go into hurricane-damaged areas and inspect buildings. I was to prepare estimates the insurance company would then use to make payments on. I wasn't going to be an insurance adjuster, just the guy who wrote the estimates.

They needed people right away, and it was important I could travel and stay gone for a few weeks because there was lots to do and even more storms on the way. We briefly discussed pay which was about four times what I had been making, and I agreed. We shook hands, and Charlie introduced me to his son, Chuck, who promptly had the girls print me out a per-diem check. Once the check was ready, he took me to the Delta ticketing office up the street to get my plane ticket. It was explained that my phone card and business cards would come in the mail in a few days. By the time I walked back to my car that afternoon, I had a one-way plane ticket to Gulf Port, Mississippi, and a five hundred dollar per diem check. I didn't even know what per-diem meant, but at least I had five hundred of them.

The night before the interview, Allison and I talked about the travel. Not knowing any specifics, we could only speak in generalities. We agreed the travel wasn't an issue as we had hardly been seeing each other lately anyway. She was working at UPS throwing boxes at 3 a.m., and I was off to construction sites by 5 a.m. We had some free time in the evening, but after dinner was made and Keller had his bath, there was little family time left before we had to be in bed to start anew for the next day. To make the travel work, we could have a friend of Allison's come to stay at the house while I was gone to help with Keller. We did not know how much the new job would pay, but we had decided it had to be enough to cover the new childcare, or it wasn't worth it. Having just received the offer, I had to let my current job know I was quitting that afternoon. While not happy about the short notice, my old job seemed to understand, especially when you considered the difference in pay. The blow of my leaving was also softened by my having a great replacement lined up to take my place. That replacement would work for them in my old role for several years, and I suspect everyone was grateful for how it all worked out.

The next problem to solve was figuring out what to pack. I had neglected to ask what the dress code was, but all of the guys in the office when I interviewed were very causal, so I took that as my cue. We had to borrow a suitcase from Allison's mom. It was a floral number with four tiny wheels at the bottom and one of those dog leash-type tethers to drag it around with. I packed boots, a hardhat, some jeans, a few t-shirts, and a polo shirt. I would later find out I had forgotten a belt and only had four pairs of socks. I still didn't know much about what I was doing. All I knew was I was flying to the airport and would meet some guy named Smith. It was late by the time everything was packed, so we went to bed, both scared and excited for what would come next. The following day, Allison took me to the airport and dropped me off. We kissed and said our goodbyes. I had elected for comfort that day as I would be flying, and the weather was going to be in the nineties when I landed. I clutched my plane ticket, and per-diem check tightly as I walked towards security. It would be three more days until I figured out what to do with that per-diem check. I thought it was somehow for me to give to the guy I was meeting to pay for my expenses. I didn't even realize it was for me to use for food while traveling. Had I realized that, I might have thought to cash it or deposit it before leaving.

Several hours later, I got off the airplane in Gulfport, Mississippi. I was meeting a guy named Smith. I saw a few people holding signs with various names on them, but none had my name. I asked the information desk, but they also had no messages or info for me. I was patient—or at least I tried to be. I called the office and, after a few tries, was able to get a hold of Chuck. He said he would figure out what was going on and let me know. I called him back a little later, and he said they were waiting for me that morning before my flight got in but not to worry, they would send a car over for me. I saw various taxis and black sedans drive by with names written on cards in the corner of the window—maybe I was looking for one of them. I watched as they passed, reading each name, never finding one that matched mine. I got a call from Chuck, and he said they were pulling up in a gold car. The only gold vehicle I could see was a limo with metallic-gold paint and a bright white vinyl roof. It couldn't be—he didn't mean that car, did he? About that time, the limo stopped in front of me and rolled down the window. Inside the vehicle were three or four sophisticated men in their forties and fifties wearing suites, and sure enough, one was named Smith. I don't know who was more shocked, them or me.

The driver helped me get my floral print bag loaded into the limo's trunk. Once the bag was secured, I was introduced to the client, Sir Richard Smith of Canada. He wasn't actually a Sir, but you would never know it. He had a strong British accent and spoke in one of the most polished manners I have ever heard. His associates were slightly younger. Shawn, who was Richard's right-hand man, and Brad, who was a senior partner at a very well know forensic accounting firm. The four of us sat in the back of this limo and did our best to make conversation. Quickly sensing I was under dressed, I shared that I had been told we weren't starting inspections until the following day, so please excuse my attire. Richard responded, "Well, we didn't expect you to be wearing short pants; regular trousers will do for next time." I spent the remainder of the car ride along and the day trying to talk as little as possible and learn quickly. They would occasionally ask for specific prices of products or services, and the best I could do was say, "normally, they would be X, but in this situation, I'm sure it will be much more." I somehow managed to bluff my way through the day.

We rode back to the hotel together, and I was faced with my first genuine hurdle. I didn't have a room. Richard's younger associate picked up on that right away and came to the rescue. He gave me the unused reservation of his colleague who was supposed to arrive a few days later. As I was checking in, I was faced with my second challenge in as many minutes; they wanted a credit card for the room. I didn't have a credit card. I had a debit card, but I only had three or four hundred dollars in the account total, and that room was more than three hundred dollars a night. On top of that, Allison would need that money to live off until I got paid. I was starting to panic, trying to figure out how I could get a room at the Best Western instead. I offered to have my boss call there in the morning to sort it out. Shawn stepped in again and said, "Just leave it on my card; give her your card for the incidentals." I didn't know what those were either, but I handed over my card anyway, trusting the process to work out. Shawn mentioned the client would get billed for it regardless, and it didn't matter. Having understood zero of the implications of that statement, I just said, "Oh, OK." As we walked away from the front desk, Shawn said, "You can't wear that tomorrow. You need to be at least wearing khakis and a nice shirt." I said OK and slowly walked up to the elevator, inventorying my wardrobe in my head.

We had a few hours until we would meet for dinner downstairs, and I needed to do some quick shopping. Luckily for me, there was a Macy's nearby I could walk to, and I was able to grab two pairs of Khakis and a dress shirt before they closed. That little trip alone cost more than a hundred dollars. I was able to make it back in time for dinner, and all was well. I came downstairs wearing my new outfit, looking like I had almost fit in. I even commented, "And you guys thought I only brought short pants," to which they all erupted. I survived my first day, but just barely. It was luck and generosity that got me through it. I was going to have to string a lot more of those days together if I was going to make it work.

The next day certainly went better than the first, and we had meetings in the morning in which I took great notes despite not understanding ninety percent of what I was noting. We didn't have any actual site inspections scheduled until the next day, so I was just trying to get the lay of the land. I did pick up on one thing, and that was this client was a chain of mortuaries and associated businesses spanning the entire gulf coast, and they had heavy losses to 130+ facilities. Around lunch that day, I got a call from Allison. She had just gotten done picking up Keller after her shift. She asked me what was wrong in a concerned tone; confused, I responded, "Nothing's wrong; why?" She said the checking account was overdrawn. There were two charges, one for the Marriott for $250 and another for Macy's for $120, which cost us another $75 in fees we didn't have. She had enough cash to get her through for a few days, but she pressed me to figure out when I was getting paid and reminded me to give that per-diem check to whoever so we could maybe get a refund on the hotel charges. We said our goodbyes and hung up so as to not waste minutes on our cell phone plan.

The second day went much better than the first. In the hotel lobby, Shawn had mentioned I had done a decent job that day and to keep it up. I took that opportunity to ask him to whom

I should give the per-diem check. I had figured out that he worked for a different company than I did, and my company worked for him. I had just assumed someone else from my company would be arriving at some point I would be reporting to and helping. Shawn paused and looked at me, tilting his head like the RCA dog before patiently explaining my engagement logistics. He told me the per-diem check was for me to deposit in my account and use to cover my meals that weren't business-related. He also explained if the meals or expenses were for the completion of the project, they would be ultimately paid by my company and then billed to the client—which was him—and he would combine those billings with his expenses and bill his client.

Shawn said hotels, airfare, and rental cars were usually put on a credit card provided by my company, and once the charges were final, those too would also be passed onto him and after his review to his client. He offered to leave the hotel on his credit card until my company sent my card to me. He also clarified I was the only person from my company coming and if I wanted to keep the job, I had better step it up as his boss Richard wasn't impressed. That conversation took maybe five minutes to have but probably an hour to unpack in my mind. That evening I called Allison around eight, which was already a little past her bedtime, and woke her up. I explained what Shawn had shared. She was relieved but also nervous. We hadn't contemplated my not keeping the job or possibly being replaced. I had my work cut out for me. The following day before we left for inspections, I went to the front desk, hoping to find a bank so I could get this check deposited. Instead, they cashed it right there on the spot for me. Happily surprised, I tucked that money into my wallet and proceeded to inspect my first real damages.

The damage to the Gulf Coast was devastating, like nothing I had ever seen before. I would later learn it was like nothing anyone had ever seen before, as Hurricane Katrina was the most damaging storm in at least a generation. We continued working our way from location to location, from the outside, towards the most significantly damaged building. As the week ended, Shawn informed me he was leaving in a few days and the next guys coming in behind him were not likely to be as understanding as he was, and they would expect a lot out of me. He also clarified they expected some preliminary estimates from me soon.

Every evening, I noticed that the other adjusters and estimators staying at the hotel would sit around the tables and other public areas, typing away on their laptops, flipping through pages of notes, and reviewing photographs. I had heard the program's name they were all using and understood that to be the expected standard for my work product. There was only one problem: I didn't have a laptop. They had never given me one when I was hired. My old laptop was left with my previous company as it was theirs. Formulating a plan in my mind, I told Shawn in order to get him some of the estimates before he left, I would need to get started writing them the next day instead of going to the inspections and meetings with him. He hesitated but ultimately agreed to bring me his notes and measurements from what they inspected that day.

That morning as Shawn and his team left the hotel; I made sure to look busy organizing my notes, etc. The second they left, I went in search of a computer. I found a used computer store near the hotel and called a cab to take me there. Once there, I was underwhelmed by the selection and price but found something that would work within my budget of three hundred dollars. I was back at the hotel just before noon and set up shop in the lobby, where I was when they left earlier that morning. I chose the lobby because the Internet was free versus $15 a day in my room. The lobby also had the added benefit of free, unlimited Diet Cokes and bar mix-peanut refills.

I borrowed an install disk from another insurance guy working nearby and got started… Then I got a blue screen of death, the worse fate that could befall a computer user of the 2000s. A marathon install session followed; driver updates, windows updates, reformatted drives, reinstalls, and finally, the working program. This travesty of an install took the literal remainder of the day. I had a working version of the estimating program up and running on my secondhand computer a full five minutes before Shawn, and the team walked back in that evening. They were shocked as I was sitting in the same seat I was when they had left ten hours earlier. The bartender overhearing their comments, said, "He's been there all day and hasn't moved, working like an animal."

No one asked to see my actual work product, and that was good as there wasn't any to share. They were just content that I was working towards getting the estimates done for them. That night we went to dinner as usual, and for the first time in a week, I felt like I wasn't an outsider in that group. I don't know if they started to accept me as someone who might stay around or if maybe my perception of them changed as I got more comfortable with my role.

The next day, I again worked on the estimates all day. I had to teach myself the program first, but that was relatively easy as I spoke geek, and it was a simple program similar to others I had used before. I had full estimates for six of the locations done by the end of the day. That was enough for us to close out the week and start planning for the rest of the inspections. The last night before Shawn left to go home for a week, he took me aside and said I had done rather good and they weren't sending me home, but I had almost blown it. He told me his replacement wouldn't be as understanding, and they would expect me to take them out to dinner each night, not the other way around. He handed me $300 and said he would see me in a week.

The next day, Shawn's replacement showed up. Layne was a fit, younger man who was straightforward and embodied the odd mix of formal and athletic. He had been a rugby player for sure, and I would guess that he had gone to a very fancy boarding school on the east coast. He was confident and capable, not afraid to call something what it was. As I had taken one of the available hotel reservations, Layne and I would be sharing a room that first night. This room-sharing arrangement was only temporary until he could move into Shawn's old room the following day. Remember when I said Layne could be direct? He was very direct and open with his displeasure of sharing a hotel room with me. That displeasure was only exacerbated following our first face-to-face introduction. This introduction included him walking in on me in the hotel room as I sat in just a pair of boxers, entering estimates on my bootleg computer. I was in the middle of a bathroom sink laundry session but still had work to do. He was not happy seeing me in just my "gitch," to use his words, pecking away at my computer. The next day couldn't come soon enough for Layne.

As we completed inspections the first day after Shawn left, Layne and I had dinner, and as I started to pay, he insisted that he would pick up the tab. That pattern continued the rest of the week—even during lunch when I would ordinarily be covering my tab. I don't know for sure, but I suspect knowing Layne could be a hard ass; Shawn may have talked to him and let him know my situation. It was either that or Layne had mastered the art of accumulating reward points and didn't want to lose an opportunity.

Shawn returned the next week, and as a team, we eventually assessed all 130 locations and found there to be more than forty million dollars in damages by the time it was all done. I hadn't seen that many dead bodies since I was wandering around the hospital with an orderly looking for my Mom's. The cycle of inspections and estimates continued for months. There were still a few hiccups that popped up, like when it was time for me to rent a car and I wasn't old enough; I was only twenty-four and needed to be twenty-five. Eventually, a solution was found, and the weeks turned into months. Allison was able to send me my company credit card and new per-diem checks to wherever hotels I was staying. While everyone else would leave for a break, I stayed and kept working.

I came back to Cincinnati for three days after Katrina in 2005 around Thanksgiving and then again at Christmas for two days. As it turned out, I had made the most of my trip home on

Thanksgiving and shortly after Christmas. Allison let me know we were pregnant with Jacob. Over the next two years, I would continue working on Hurricane Katrina claims, starting with the funeral homes and progressing up the food chain, higher and higher. By the time I was done with Katrina work, I had handled some of the most significant claims of the entire storm and my career. I was never really the right guy for the job. There were always better consultants with more technical understanding, better education, more experience, and sometimes all three. However, I still somehow found myself in the right place at the right time. On top of pure luck, I always managed to deliver. I would hear parts of a discussion that went along the lines of "well, he hasn't fucked it up yet; let him keep going." I took those sentiments as both confirmation of my hard work and an explicit acknowledgment that I would be replaced if I didn't continue to perform. That threat wasn't an abstract, I knew with absolute certainty that I would be replaced if I didn't perform, and that was motivating to say the least.

Chapter 14

Death of a Legend

Once 2006 rolled around, my travel schedule for work started to taper off. I would still spend way too much time on the road, but I would try to come back for at least a long weekend each month. My absence was hard on everyone. Allison and Keller missed me something fierce, but I suspect Keller's excitement to see me was more his mirroring of mom's excitement as he hadn't ever seen me that much since he was a baby. Hailey missed me a lot as well. Whenever I came home, she would always spend the weekend with me, cramming in as many fun things and activities as we could. Allison even came to me in New Orleans during Mardi Gras that first year to combat the time away from each other. We all stayed in a fancy hotel downtown. The hotel served peanut butter and jelly sandwiches in the evening on a big platter, and they were Keller's favorite.

We went out as a family to watch the parades. Keller loved the visuals, but not so much the throwing of the beads after being hit square in the face with a set. Allison and Keller rode around with me as I showed them the city—all of the landmarks and devastation. That trip would be the start of what has evolved as a tradition in our family. Whenever I am on the road for a large disaster, the whole family just comes along for a few days. It somehow humanizes what I do and lets them see why I do it. As the kids have gotten older, it has given them a valuable perspective of just how bad something can be without all of the emotional baggage gained by earning that perspective the way I did as a child.

The trips with the family down to me were nice, but they were also the exception. I still depended on the trips back home for most of my contact with them. It was also during these trips back home that I would see Papaw. While we would talk nearly as much as Allison and I did, I didn't get to see him as often, only on the short trips back home. Those trips back could never come soon enough. I would always stop by and see him the morning after I landed, if not sooner. I would stop by his place and play with his cat, Tiger, a twenty-five-pound Bengal cat that stood as tall as most dogs, and visit his neighbor, Joe. Joe was a character for sure, essentially serving as Papaw's Darrell, offering both friendship and a little personality to boot. I would always make it a point to give Papaw money and maybe pay a bill or two if I could talk him into letting me. It was the least I could do as I had contributed significantly to his bankruptcy years before.

On one of those trips home, I noticed Papaw had lost a little weight. He looked healthy and seemed to be getting around well—his clothes just looked a little loose. He had tightened his belt to its last hole by the next trip home. I took him shopping and bought him some new clothes. That weight loss was alarming, and I urged him to get in to see the doctor. Allison and I also started cooking for him. Before I left, I bought an assortment of styrofoam trays and dishes and wrote down all of his favorite recipes that Granny made—pinto beans and cornbread, fried potatoes, sour kraut, sausages, everything. I also made sure they were made the same way with Crisco and butter, with all the right brands and styles of ingredients. Before I left that week, I had made a full week's worth of meals—breakfast, lunch, and dinner with dates and instructions for heating right on the boxes. Allison promised to check on him every few days and make sure she brought more food each time. Keep in mind at this time, Allison was three or four months pregnant with Jacob, courtesy of the 3-day homecoming the previous thanksgiving. Allison was also charged with picking Hailey up from school and watching her until Jill got off work while juggling Keller's many therapies and doctors' visits. She ran the household for an absentee father and had her hands full.

The next time I came back was three weeks later, and Papaw looked worse. At first, I accused Allison of not checking on him or taking the meals over, but she had done both. Papaw had been calling the doctors, but no one would see him, or they weren't accepting new patients. His regular doctor had retired, and the new management group at St Elizabeth dismissed him as a patient because he owed them money for previous visits or copays. He couldn't get into any other offices as a new patient because he only had Medicare, and they weren't accepting new Medicare patients that didn't have previous medical records. He couldn't get his records from the old office until the bill was paid. That night I took Papaw to the emergency room, not knowing what else to do, and after many hours they offered nothing in the way of answers. The doctors said he was dehydrated and sent us home.

Over the next several days, I got the medical records and the doctors' situation straightened out. I paid the ransom for the records and personally visited a doctor's office just a few blocks from his apartment to beg them to accept him as a patient. The office agreed to accept him, and the doctor saw him the next day. The new office had reviewed the blood work from the emergency room and ordered a new chest x-ray. Within a few days, I had a phone call. The doctor wanted to meet with us at her office. I had hoped it would be a quick catch-up and status update, but I was also realistic. I had never heard of meeting a doctor outside of an appointment for good news. That meeting was no exception to the rule. Papaw—who had chronic emphysema and had been a smoker his whole life—had cancer of the esophagus, likely contributed by the menthol cigarettes and persistent heartburn he had since I was a child. They were referring him to a specialist, but it appeared from the x-ray and lab work it had spread and was terminal.

Papaw's reaction to that news was quite different from mine. I was angry with the delays in finding it and wanted to take action to get the best treatments and procedures. Papaw was quick to minimize it. For a long time, I thought he was in denial about the diagnosis and how bad it was. He told his buddy Joe that it might be a little spot of cancer, and they would have to do more tests—that was decidedly not true. It was cancer, and they knew that because they had done the tests. At that time, I felt very alone and looked to Allison for help, the problem was that she didn't have much to give me. Allison was five months pregnant and still balancing all her previous responsibilities, and now I was dropping this on her. I was trying to figure out how we could have Papaw come live with us, but I knew that wouldn't be practical. Our house had steps everywhere—three at the front door, two in the garage, and a whole flight to get to a bathroom. On top of that, Keller had grown into an autistic, sensory-craving, partially deaf, speech-impaired kid that received any number of occupational and speech therapies at the house several days a week. On top of everything else, Allison was deeply afraid that Jacob would be just like Keller was with the crying and lack of sleeping when he arrived. Papaw—still fully mentally present—also saw the difficulties of this situation and suggested getting a nurse to come to his apartment or possibly an assisted living apartment.

The problem with all of the half-measures was they didn't fit into a neat definition. He was too sick for a nurse that would just stop by but not sick enough for a full nursing home. His condition was getting worse too quickly for assisted living to be practical, but a nursing home was still a little way away. Ultimately what he needed was something that I couldn't accept at first—hospice. I had been home for almost a month and had to leave. Allison was getting more pregnant every day, and Papaw was getting sicker. We agreed to decide as soon as I got back, but we all knew it to be a certainty more than a possibility.

When I got back that next time, it was about July, and luckily there would only be a few shorter trips in the coming months. Some of my claims had settled and my projects were wrapping up. It was perfect timing; I could spend more time helping around the house and with Papaw. When I went to see Papaw, I was surprised, he was looking good. The daily trips by Allison to check on him and make sure he had healthy food were helping. He had gained three pounds and looked better overall. The cancer specialist had gotten a chance to see him and had him set up to start chemotherapy as soon as he gained a little more weight. It was not all good news, however. His strength had faded even more, and he struggled to walk most of the time.

He was not going to be able to stay in his apartment anymore. There was a bed opening up at a rehab center that would be a good fit as we marched towards the inevitable. He would still be able to be as independent as he wanted to be with visitors and the ability to leave the center if he desired. He would also have nurses to help him and easy transport for treatment and doctors' visits. He agreed to go but was hesitant. Papaw and I made arrangements to smuggle in cash and an ID that he kept in a travel wallet that he wore around his neck. I also gave him a second cell phone with everyone's numbers pre-programmed in case he needed to escape and he couldn't get to his phone. We planned it so if he wanted to break out, he could tell us, and we would come to the center and tell them he had a doctor's appointment, and we would just take him.

All of that planning was, of course, unnecessary in a practical sense. However, in some ways, it was an absolute necessity. Creating the theater and allusion was necessary for both Papaw and I to accept that next step. Call it a rehab center, a nursing home, or hospice—it was likely going to be where he went to die. We knew that in both our minds, but if there were hope or even a possibility that wouldn't be the case, we would hang onto that scrap of hope and even embrace it through hidden cash and escape plans. I don't know if there was a single day that went by in the following weeks, that he didn't have at least one visitor. I did everything I could to get long-lost friends and family to stop by, essentially to return the favor of his previous unannounced visits so many years before. By the end of August, Allison was very pregnant, much of my work had wrapped up, and I was ready for a bit of downtime. Papaw had gained a little more weight and was prepared to have his first round of chemotherapy. The goal of the treatments wasn't to cure him but to maybe push back some of the cancer that was causing the worst symptoms.

Jacob was late, establishing the beginnings of what would become a pattern that still exists to this day. The due date came and went, and it was time to induce labor and get him out before he overcooked. I had arranged my travel to be home the entire week before and after Jacob was due to arrive. I thought I had covered all of my bases. The only problem was a big meeting in New York on the 22nd that I couldn't miss, and Jacob still hadn't arrived. Allison's labor was induced on August 21st, 2006, and after a few false starts and an eventual C-section, Jacob Tyler White graced us with his presence. That night, Jacob slept on my bare chest, barely making a move or crying, while mom recovered in the bed next to us. That morning, I left the hospital and went directly to the airport.

Having just held my son for the first time eight hours before, I was on my way to a conference room on the 42nd floor in the McGraw Hill building. I spent my day and night in New York City, making it back just in time to pick up Allison and Jacob from the hospital. Based on Allison's account, the second night didn't go as smoothly as the first, with Jacob being very hungry and their mom unable to nurse no one was happy. Allison had developed a fever the second day and was shaking with chills by the evening. The nurses, recognizing she was alone, pitched in and helped her get some sleep that night with the help of antibiotics. When Allison and I got home that Wednesday morning, we were both exhausted and happy to sleep in our own bed for the first time in three days. The next morning she was feeling better, having beat back the infection, but was still exhausted.

The next few days went by so quickly. Everyone wanted to see the baby, including Keller and Hailey. We all pitched in to help and let mom have some rest. That Friday was Papaw's first chemotherapy session, and I was planning on bringing him by the house on the way home so he could see baby Jacob.

Friday morning came, and I took Keller with me so Allison only had Jacob to worry about. She continued working all morning as she got the house cleaned up and ready for Papaw. By that time, Keller still wasn't talking, but he had some partial words I could understand, and between eye contact and a few hand signs,(learned from Ray) we could get along pretty well. We picked up Papaw and went to the chemo center. There was a lot of paperwork and waiting as it was Papaw's first session. That delay wasn't a good fit for Keller's energy at the time which was hovering around the level of a monkey on amphetamines. Papaw was infinitely patient with him and said I was just like that when I was little, and I somehow didn't doubt that. When I conceived my master plan to bring Keller to the injection site, I wasn't aware it would take an hour or more just to do the injection. Once they got Papaw in the back and hooked up, I excused myself to run Keller back home. It wasn't a long trip, and I would be back before the IV had finished. I was on my way back to the chemo site, maybe ten minutes when I got a call from them. I had left my number, but I didn't think I had taken too long I was wondering why they were calling me. The nurse told me Papaw had reacted to the drugs, and the life squad had taken him over to the ER, which was only a mile or so away. My adrenaline started to peak. I called Allison and told her to have someone watch the kids and get to the hospital as soon as possible. Luckily a friend of hers had stopped by, and she would soon be on her way.

I walked into the ER and was directed back to a room where I could see Papaw surrounded by a lot of commotion. This surprised me as we had already filed a DNR back when he first went into the rehab center. The second he saw me, he sat up, pulling himself towards me by grabbing the bed rails, and said,

"There he is." He had been waiting for me. The doctors told me he had a cardiac event in reaction to the chemo injection, and that his heart rate was unstable. I helped them understand that the focus of his treatment should be on comfort, and they clearly understood the subtext. I spent the next twenty minutes comforting him and holding him in my arms. I had crawled up into the bed next to him and held him in my arms as he slipped away. I reminded him he would get to see Granny and my Mom, that his Mom and Dad were there waiting for him, and so was Billie. I comforted him and told him everything was going to be all right. I told him how much I loved him and how good of a job he did taking care of me. In those last moments with him, I somehow had a freeness of spirit that helped me share every emotion and connection with him. I am eternally grateful for that opportunity. Just as Papaw was taking his last struggling breaths, Allison showed up to say her goodbyes and comfort me.

Russell Lee Hodge died on August 25th, 2006. He was two weeks shy of his 74th birthday. He is survived by his one SON, Justin White, and three grandkids, Hailey, Keller, and Jacob.

Papaw died having never met Jacob. They only shared this world together for a few days, never touching or even seeing each other. Papaw certainly would remember his time with Keller. Unfortunately, Keller was a little too young to remember him. Lacking significant and severe trauma, kids don't usually remember stuff when they are that young. While I regret Keller never knowing Papaw, at least I know it's for the right reasons. Hailey does have memories of him. As Jill and Hailey lived in the same apartment complex as him, it was common for her to see him and visit some days when they would feed the ducks. Hailey and Papaw got more time together than I ever knew, which warms my heart. I also found out later that Jill even visited him in the rehab center just to say hello, dropping by unannounced in the same way as was his custom.

The Monday after he died, we started making arrangements for his funeral; he always said he wanted someone to dig a post hole and drop him in. While I understood his sentiment, that was not practical nor deserved after the kind and generous life he had lived. There was one peculiar quirk to making the arrangements. I was now a funeral industry pro, and while it was my primary role to assess the damages, I couldn't help but have picked up a thorough understanding of the business practices along the way. I suspect that dollar-for-dollar, Papaw's funeral was the least profitable one given that year by the funeral industry as a whole. I somehow saw it as my duty to show Papaw one last time just how good I could do and what I learned from the expensive education he'd bought me. Papaw is buried to the right of his loving wife. He lies with her, sharing the same shade of the dogwood tree shared with Billie and my Mom.

Chapter 15

It Might Not be Beverly Hills But We are Hillbillies

A few months after Papaw died, my life would take another turn. That turn wasn't as dramatic as others, but it certainly was a course plotted in a new direction. On nearly the same whim as I had started this career, I took a new job in Chicago. I would be doing very much the same job and have the same responsibilities; what was different was it would be for a much more technical firm, and I would be living in the big city. It was an easy choice in some ways as it was for even better pay and more opportunity, but it also meant leaving Hailey behind with her mom. That was the biggest challenge with accepting the offer. Mathematically it meant I had about four days a year less with Hailey than the current visitation allowed, but in reality, as I wouldn't be on long deployments, I would get to spend real time with her. Jill was stubborn, but we eventually agreed Hailey would reside primarily in KY still but would come up to Chicago during all school breaks and on the holidays of Easter and Thanksgiving. As I mentioned, that wasn't a massive change in the number of days, just the grouping of the days. On top of the planned schedule, Allison and I planned to come back to KY often to visit with her family and get the boys time with grandma and grandpa.

We moved to the suburb of Lake Forest, located north of

Chicago, in the fall of 2006. My office was downtown, and due to traffic, I quickly learned it was most efficient to take the train every morning. This unfamiliar environment shocked both Allison and I on many levels. We knew little about Chicago and were on a quick time frame to find a new place to live. Every time we found the perfect house or area, there would always be some underlying problem—bad schools, high crime, a terrible commute, etc. Growing frustrated during the search, I surveyed nearly anyone I could find and asked them what one neighborhood, no matter what house or block you chose, would generally be acceptable. Repeatedly, I got the same response "Lake Forest" but I didn't fully understand the magnitude of those answers. It was basically like asking strangers the question all across the US, and people responded with 90210. Yes, Beverly Hills is lovely, but can you imagine what it would be like living there? Lake Forest is the Beverly Hills of Chicago, and it was no small feat to find a place within our budget in that town, but we did. It was small, but it had three bedrooms and a great finished basement for the boys to play in. We shared a yard, but it was only half a block from a park. The train station was only a short drive or bike ride away, and when the weather was nice, we could walk to a private beach on Lake Michigan.

I loved Lake Forest. Allison, not so much. One of the difficulties she faced was while I got to go into the city every day and work, she was stuck at home with the boys. Now she certainly wasn't stuck, but it did mean every interaction she had with other adults revolved around the kids. Trips to the park, walks down to the beach, getting ice cream at the little shop in town. That doesn't sound bad, but—and you know there's a but—none of the adults were the parents of the kids. They were the nannies or hired help. The seemingly innocuous question of what family you are with was code for whose nanny are you. Nannies, no matter how professional or casual, will never interact with parents the same way as they would with other nannies. It's like how the crew is never supposed to be above deck unless they are working on a cruise, and the passengers are never supposed to be below deck to see the real crew's life. In Lake Forest, Allison felt like she had snuck downstairs every day, and people were looking at her. In the evenings, if we tried to interact socially, it was the opposite, almost like we were the "help" trying to mingle with the first-class passengers. Even when people knew they were our kids, we suddenly had to deal with a pretty steep age gap between Allison—who was early to mid-twenties—and the average resident of Lake Forest, who was forty-eight years old. On top of age, there was the issue of employment. Only a third had regular jobs, but somehow, we're still able to maintain a median income in excess of one hundred and seventy thousand dollars a year. It was a place for old, rich people, not young, hardworking, but middle-class families.

There were some exceptions to our exile on the island of age and income. A guy and his daughter would walk by all the time and became friends with the boys and Allison. We would often talk and socialize. I figured he felt a lot like we did. He was around our same age and had a child about the same age as Jacob. The only difference was he was the most recognizable linebacker in Chicago. My complete blindness to sports meant he could have regular conversations and interactions that didn't revolve around his job. I hope he appreciated this, as we certainly enjoyed the rarity of getting to know other young families that struggled to fit in just like we did.

That summer, when Hailey came up, she had a fun time. We had enrolled her in summer camp, and there was a bus that would pick her up each morning. She spent the day with the other campers in the woods and going to the beach. I look back on these times with fondness and remorse, as that summer was ultimately going to be a preview of what life would become for Hailey. Jill had come up to Chicago to drop Hailey off at the beginning of the summer. We had anticipated this being a chance for Jill to see the house and feel comfortable with the neighborhood and situation. We had expected we would all go to dinner before Jill started the long drive back. Instead, Jill dropped Hailey off after what seemed like the most extended road trip in history, with detours and confusion mixed in. Jill spent maybe fifteen minutes making small talk and saying goodbye. She asked for the promised gas money, and she was off. That interaction left Allison and me with a slight tinge of a feeling but nothing specific. At the time, I tried to chalk it up to Chicago traffic and a difficult day. It seems it might have been the very beginning of what would be a long couple of years for everyone involved.

We would ultimately spend about eighteen months living in Chicago. My love for the city remained consistent, but Allison's tolerance began to fade. It started with her taking more and more weekend trips back to Kentucky. At first, I would go on all of them and then resorted to letting her stretch and combine weekends with me traveling in between. The final straw was a weekend trip she had planned to Kentucky. That week, we argued about mundane and boring stuff—money, sex, household chores—standard three or four-year marriage growing pain stuff. I came home early that Friday, intent on surprising her and going back to Kentucky with her. She was happy to see me, and it was good news I was coming with her as she hated the long drive. The problem came when I started to pack my things and found she had already way over packed for a single weekend trip. She hadn't been planning on moving out for good, but it was clear she was planning on staying longer than a few days. The drive to Kentucky was particularly awkward that week.

In my life, I sometimes tend to get hyper-focused on specific ideas or tasks while ignoring others. It has always been a problem, and it has seemed to be getting worse for many years. My marriage and our living in Chicago were no different. While I was focusing on making a new life in a big city, I ignored Allison and my family. Not from the sense of spending time with them—that part was good as we only had each other. Instead, I was ignoring them in the sense of what was best for them and what was their actual state of mind and needs. The boys were thriving. Keller had been getting excellent medical care and was now talking and making substantial progress with the healing of his ears. While Hailey was happy with us that summer, the truth was she missed everything about home when she was with us. She was essentially faced with trading time with her mom and the baby sister to spend time with her brothers and me. Neither were terrible options; it wasn't fair that it could only be one or the other. Allison was profoundly unhappy on the inside. She had been ripped away from her family, and everything she knew in exchange for a place she could see made me happy. She put on a happy face, did the best she could, and successfully hid her pain, but it was still there. It was hard, but it was what was best for my family in the end. We moved back to Kentucky.

In the end, I still look at our time in Chicago very differently than Allison. I think it was good for us. We finally had a period in which we could only rely on each other. There was no getting bailed out by her mom or Papaw anymore. If there was a problem, it was up to us to work it out. Allison became much more confident and capable and grew as a mother and partner during that time. To hear Allison's perspective, she threw herself into faking it in the hope we could eventually make it, and the false persona would become a reality. One thing is for sure; I never knew how heartbroken Allison was until we came back. It was only through seeing her back in KY and thriving that I could see how unhappy she had been in Chicago. When I view it objectively, coming back was right for us. On top of tremendously improving things between Allison and I, it allowed us to be there for the coming storm involving Hailey.

At that point, it was the spring of 2008, just a day or two after Hailey's sister's birthday. I had gotten a call from Jill that was pivotal, to say the least. She asked if it would be okay if Hailey stayed with us for a few days because Emma, Hailey's little sister, was in the hospital. I responded, of course, she could, but more importantly, I asked how we could help and what had happened with Emma. That is where everything changed. After Emma's birthday party, Hailey and her were playing in the car when it was knocked out of gear. Fearing for Emma's safety, Hailey tried to get Emma out of the car by throwing her out.

Unable to get her far enough away from the car, it had run over her, and Emma had broken her femur. That conversation left a lot to unpack, but the essential parts were Emma's birthday party, Hailey throwing Emma to safety, Emma being run over, and having a broken leg. The most problematic part was that this event had happened following Emma's party, two days before the call I was getting, and that they had just gone to the hospital late the night before, a full day and a half after the accident. Rest assured, my spidey sense was on fire; I made arrangements to go get Hailey from her house that afternoon, where Jill's aunt was watching her. Hailey ended up living with us from that day forward. While that day set everything into motion, it would take another four years for there to be any finality to the long-drawn-out journey it was. There would be various levels of shared custody, visitation, and even supervision during those four years. In the end, each level of escalation on our part was to protect Hailey further and had a corresponding deepening of the issues facing Jill as a cause. When everything was done, it became clear there had been a progressing addiction, starting with over-the-counter diet pills and ending with full-blown heroin dependency eight years later. The only thing I want to say further about Jill was she was an amazing mom who loved all of her kids. Before the addiction, she was selfless and dedicated. Even during the addiction, she cared for her children. She took extraordinary steps of self-sacrifice to ensure that what was ultimately best for the children could happen for them—even if that meant she couldn't have them or be there for them herself.

Hailey living with us full-time wasn't the only change in our life after moving back from Chicago. Our now larger family needed a permanent place to call home. AT first, we had been living in a cute three-bedroom in a suburb at the end of a cul-de-sac. Allison loved that house, but it wasn't ours, and it was time to find our kids a forever home as they would be starting school soon. We found ourselves first looking in a familiar area—Burlington, the very same small town I grew up in. It had the advantage of a low cost of living and a neat feel but lacked the great schools and more contemporary homes we were looking for. We finally settled on a house in the next town over. It had great schools, five bedrooms, a nice garage for me, and was close to the airport, which was a great convenience. We moved into that home in the summer of '09. It was the cheapest house in the best neighborhood, and it was ours, dated decor and all. Allison set to work making it a home, and I found myself living minutes away from the very streets and neighborhood I grew up in. This proximity to the area of my childhood and teenage years would be the genesis of a twist of fate that would reunite me with my long-lost brother.

I was getting gas at the local station when I heard someone say, "Hey, Justin, it's Jason." I turned around to see Jason Strange. He was always part of my inner circle back in the day, from my failed attempts at high school through the paintball days. Jason had has ultimately become Scott's best friend as I migrated to Darrell, but we were all very much intertwined growing up. We caught up a little, exchanged information, and agreed to have lunch the next day. The following day, Jason and I met for lunch. Since then, we have spent hours reminiscing about old times and hearing about each other's adventures and journeys. At some point, the topic turned to Darrell. Jason was fully aware of all that had transpired ten years prior, having had the unique privilege of perhaps seeing both sides as he was a relatively neutral party in the whole affair. Knowing that, he let me know that he and Darrell would occasionally talk, and sometimes I had even been the topic of the conversation. Jason filled me in on Darrell and his marriage, how his parents were doing, and that he was living on a farm not too far away. We closed that particular topic of conversation with Jason by saying, "You really should reach out to him. I know he'd be glad to hear from you." That lunch lasted another forty-five minutes, with us parting ways and agreeing to stay in touch. I remember thinking it was nice reconnecting with Jason and marveling at how much some things had changed and how so much was just as I had left it so many years before. Over the next week or two, I kept thinking back to that conversation with Jason. I even spoke to Allison about it and how I did miss Darrell. The biggest problem was I still didn't dare to confront my past head-on. What would I say to him? How would I start a conversation so many years later when I had some much responsibility that had never been fully settled? I'm not sure what the tipping point was precise.

I don't know if it was running into other people I had learned in that previous life or if maybe inside I knew I had to do something or it would eat at me for another ten years. Still lacking the courage to just drop by his house while also unsure how my presence would be received, I decided to write Darrell a letter. In the letter, I took full responsibility for everything we had already known. I added a few details to give him some context as to how things went between Ray and Papaw. That letter, in many ways, followed the account I gave earlier in this book, as I had a copy of it in front of me when I wrote the previous chapter. While I am not comfortable sharing the specific letter with a broader audience, it is fair to say I surrendered to his mercy and apologized. I left it up to Darrell regarding the next steps and put the letter in the mail.

About three days later, I received a call from Darrell. He had gotten the letter and wanted me to come down to his house and see him. While I didn't know precisely how our meeting would go based on the call, I was confident it wouldn't lead to my demise. I hopped in my truck and headed to his farm. As I drove the fourteen minutes to his farm, many things rushed through my head—the RC car memories, the escape, the fire, each coming faster and faster until before I knew it, I was there. As is the custom, I pulled up the gravel driveway slowly to not rut the gravel and stir up dust. When I pulled up to the barn, he stood outside, holding court amongst some of his friends and his brother-in-law. He was still tall as ever, with a slightly less mullety mullet coming down just to his neckline. White t-shirt and jeans were still his uniform, and he had sunglasses on his head, but not his signature Oakley's. His face hadn't changed much since I had seen him last—maybe a little more worn, but not by much, certainly no more than mine had. As I stepped out of my truck and walked toward him, he stopped his current conversation, walked towards me with a smile, and extended his extended arm, his hand ready to shake. We shook hands and ultimately hugged the ways guys do—first with the grasp and then a half-hug half-huddle move. We spent another fifteen to twenty minutes catching up. I saw his wife, who I have known since middle school. She recounted how excited he was to get the letter from me, probably relaying details he would have never shared on his own.

After that brief catch-up, he said, "We're heading to the demolition derby at the fair; let's go." He didn't ask if I wanted to go, he just knew I would go, and I did exactly that. In less than twenty minutes, ten years of pain had been erased. We picked up right where we left off, just a little older and wiser than we had been. We both had careers and families, responsibilities and pressures. Still, in the end, none of that mattered because we had each other again, and history had proven we could make it through just about anything.

Since our reunion, we have remained each other's best friends. I don't even know that we haven't always been each other's best friends—we just had ten years of disagreement. We don't always have the same frequency of visits or interactions as life tends to get in the way, but every time we talk or see each other, not a single second has passed since the last. We have spoken from time to time about how we felt during the years apart, and the common theme for both of us is sadness we weren't there for each other when we both needed a friend. I regret not being around for his wedding and the growth of his business, and he regrets not being there when Papaw died or as I was just starting my family. No matter our regrets, we both, through our experience, have a firmer understanding of what it means to appreciate the things in life that matter, like friends and family, and that it is never too late or too far to retrieve the friends and family you thought you may have lost.

Looking back on everything that happened with Darrell, I certainly have regrets. There is nothing I can do now to change the past; I can only move forward. That's precisely what I did by writing the letter. I decided to accept the past for what it was and just do what I could to move forward. That attitude and approach have been frequented in my life. This isn't a good thing. I think everyone would agree it's a lot easier to have not broken something in the first place than it is to try to fix it. While better than nothing, there isn't a lot of nobility in going about fixing things and moving past stuff that's your fault in the first place. Part of the problem is I have learned there is no guarantee you will get an opportunity to fix something. I never got the chance to fix things with my mom—the last time I saw her, I was crushing her mailbox for spite. What I wouldn't do to be able just to write a letter and tell her I was sorry. Imagine if I hadn't run into Jason at the gas station to take it a step further—would I have ever written Darrell that letter? Maybe not. I would have always felt the same way about the situation, but the ability to fix it would have been lost.

Chapter 16

Replacement Thinking

I served as the replacement child for my grandparents. I took the place of Billie not only in a physical sense but in the sense of giving them a do-over. I gave them another shot; they knew they would never get him back, but now they had me. I was going to get every advantage they had wanted for Billie but had not been able to give him. My presence truly was a gift to them in so many ways—a distraction, an outlet, a chance to grieve. However, I didn't come only bearing the gift of replacement; I also served as a reminder. I was a puzzle piece that almost fit but not quite. When they should have been enjoying retirement, I instead had them going to pewee football games and playing catch.

Their experiences and fears came into play when raising me; I suspect that if Granny and Papaw had watched Billie get into trouble with something they would steer me away from the same mistake without even realizing it. Ultimately, I served as a replacement for Billie, but I was never Billie, not to them, not to anyone, not even those in need of him the most. I could never be him, no matter how strongly others on the outside desired. Inevitably, I had a lot of the same traits and experiences as Billie as I was raised by the same people and shared his DNA. I played with the same toys and walked the same streets. I was, of course, going to be like him, but that didn't make me him.

Everyone had wanted and expected wonderful things from him, just as they do from any child. As a grandson, I was subject to the same lofty expectations. I believe that nothing about this part of how I grew up was out of the ordinary. What was different had nothing to do with them. It had to do with how I developed from experiencing extraordinary events while subject to average circumstances. It was not the family who made me the replacement son; it was me.

Either consciously or unconsciously, I wanted to help them heal and wanted to fill any openings or gaps I could. Imagine a small child seeing their mother sad—what would that child not do? What behavior would they not adopt if it meant their mom was a little less sad? That is where I excelled; I saw those opportunities and openings, and I melded myself to whatever shape or form was needed. If Granny was patriarchal, then I was obedient. If she was apt to seek sympathy, then I would give it. No one made me do something; I chose those paths, however misguided they may have ended up being.

As I got older, I mentioned I was subject to expectations. The funny thing about expectations is they are quickly adapted and changed when left alone. I kept coming up against the same expectations because I was reinforcing them and guiding them—not the other way around. When someone called me Crazy, I felt ashamed, but I kept acting Crazy. I had made the bargain with myself that the positives easily outweighed any negatives I felt with the name. I didn't start having real issues with the expectations and my associated behavior until it negatively affected my life. When that happened, I reinvented myself as an uber-geek in the same pattern as before in a slightly dressed-up form. I replaced one version of myself with another. The choice to do so was based, in fact, but also based on practicality; it was easier and quicker just to become someone they needed me to be rather than deal with who I was.

As I got older, this process refined itself. Instead of completely changing who I was to fit someone's needs, I started to change parts of who I was. This further evolved into adjusting smaller and smaller pieces of who I was to match any given requirement. This, however, had a limit as once you change too many things, you start to lose any authenticity tied to who you really are. This limit on changing yourself ultimately serves as a reality check. While some can meld and adapt more than others, no one can completely transform into something else. When people take this adaptation too far, they find real-life consequences. Examples of this are people who exude abundance and confidence but can only do so while blogging from their parent's basement. People can sometimes travel so far from who their authentic self is that they cease to exist as real people and only exist as false, constructed shells.

If you can't infinitely change yourself, how can you get past these traumas that make you who you are? To get past the traumas, you first have to know them. I want to clarify that this collection of my experiences was not meant as an endless series of trauma porn or "one-up-manship." If you want to read about the truly depraved and neglectful things humans can do to one another, there are many stories far worse than mine. It is also important to point out that everyone develops their own trauma scale from their own experiences and perceptions. One person's "worst day of my life" may be very different than another's, but it can still be objectively true for both of them. There is no chance to temper or define how bad someone's worst day is in a relative sense. It stands alone as their worst day without the need for a yardstick of comparison.

What exists as someone's worst day at a single point in time is also subject to change. An obvious way it can change is from a more significant event occurring that displaces the former. A less obvious change could be the addition of new context or perceptions that serve to redefine existing traumas. It is possible that the death of someone's pet could occupy the top spot on their list until one day they learn those long tender back rubs shared between a favorite uncle weren't as delicate or confined to the back as they initially remembered. Nothing changed about the events—both happened in the past, but it wasn't until there was some change in perception that the person was able to realize their worse day just got redefined. Now replace "Worst Day" with "Trauma," and you will start to see how memories can get tricky.

This redefining of the "worst day" or "trauma" of the events I shared is very much subject to the same scenario of reshuffling and redefining. While I have taken great pains to capture the events accurately (T), my recollection of the details is still subject to the lens of my perception (t). These lenses tint everything I remember. More importantly, what these events represent in terms of impact on me changes over time. An easy example of the change in impact is found inside the events related to the paintball store and how I viewed my grandfather's investment in it. One perfectly reasonable view could be that I squandered his money like a child and justified it through delusion. Another argument could be that it served as a very generous and appropriate gift of an education that was precisely tailored to my needs in a way that a traditional college might not have been able to do.

The truth is that both are true. I believed I had wasted his money for a sizable portion of the years since the store closed, and it was my fault he was broke. I carried shame and guilt for a long time despite him telling me otherwise many times. It has only been in the last five years that I have been able to view the circumstances in the way I shared with you. Both versions are objectively true. It is not the actual events that changed; it is only my understanding of them and how they impacted me that has changed. The same thing can be said about nearly every one of my traumas; how they have affected me has evolved and changed over time. It is also important to point out that we as humans are a sum of all our experiences, good and bad, and those experiences determine how we interpret events in our future. The experiences can't change, but the new experiences can very much redefine how we interpret and feel about the previous events. I want to share something that has helped me decipher what was and is real and what was simply perception. It is based on the water fountain in Burlington I used to visit as a child.

The Allegory of the Water Fountain

As a child, I remember the best water fountain in the world. On a sweltering summer day, you could go into the cold, air-conditioned building and press the button. Out would flow a steady, filling stream of the coldest water you could drink. If you went too quickly, your head would ache, trying to adjust.

As an adult, you can go back to this same water fountain, where you are faced with a few possibilities.

1. Is the water fountain still there, and is it working like it used to? Have the settings changed, or was it replaced with a newer model?

2. Is the water fountain still in place and still operating precisely as it did when you were a child? Is the stream as robust, and is the temperature just as cold as you remember? Has what was once exceptional become rather ordinary and mundane through the lens of time?

3. Is the water fountain still in place? While seeming worn and weathered through the years, does it still work? Does a press of the button release a stream just as strong and cold as you remember, confirming the reality in your memory was, in fact, just reality the whole time?

Which options fit you? Do different options fit different circumstances? Do you want it to be one option, but deep down, you know it's another? In my case, I went back to the very same water fountain and it was still there. I pressed the button not knowing what to expect. As I get a mouth full of water that felt as if it had come from the tip of a glacier, I had my answer. In my case, it turns out the water fountain was indeed exactly as

I remember it. That hasn't been the truth for every item I've tested. Some have been grossly wrong and others have been different but somehow still similar to my memories. I went to the apartment I grew up in and I can still see bloodstains on the wall under layers of paint and the remnants of a dent from the frying pan. At the same time, I have never been able to find anyone who actually remembers seeing Billie pushing around a 6-month-old in a stroller at the country fair. Does it matter that one event may be more true than another? I'm not sure but I know if I only focus on which one was more real I will end up spending a lot of time on something that in the end doesn't matter when I instead could be spending it with my family or helping others.

Regardless of how your experiences and traumas measure up against objective facts, they still remain true for you. It does not matter if you have a picture-perfect recollection or a delusional slant on the facts—the memories still exist. They exist, but they also assimilate into you and become part of who you are. Once in place, they are unmovable; they can be molded, reformed, and colored over as new information becomes available, but they are still there. Regardless of how you redefine and change them, they are still a part of you, good or bad, and it's up to you to decide what to do with them. I suggest you embrace them precisely as they exist today; don't rehash and try to reinvent your past but rather use them as tools as you move forward.

My experience cleaning up the blood and guts left in my Mom's trailer after her death was traumatic. But—and this is an important point. They also allowed me to approach my first assignment of a very successful career with a level of professionalism and even a bit of a superpower compared to my peers. Many of the funeral homes and embalming facilities were fully "occupied" when the floodwaters of Katrina hit the Gulf Coast. These same facilities were inaccessible for weeks following the storm and were sitting in the hot Louisiana sun. Suddenly not being shocked or paralyzed by the sights and smells of cadavers, skeletonized remains, and the reddish-brown pools of greasy decomp fluids had a real-world advantage. I could walk into a room and not flinch while others had to attack the scene in a quick burst between heaves. Because I was able to prove myself unphased by the sights and smells of my work, my assignments progressed in complexity and significance as I continued to prove myself an emotional robot.

The memories of cutting the bloodstains out of the floor of my mom's trailer still hurt and make me feel sadness and guilt for her loneliness at the time of her death. Objectively, the bad parts of sadness and guilt have a corresponding component of accomplishment. I was able to clean up the trailer at the time because I had no other option. It was a gross, dirty, and disgusting task, but it had to be done. Little did I know that same experience that once represented sadness and guilt would be transformed into pride a few years later. I had been able to turn that negative into a positive. In fact, because of it, I was able to thrive in environments that paralyzed others.

A contrasting example comes in the way I deal with police. As a child, I was exposed to police in three primary ways: Granny's blaming and hostility towards them for the death of her son, watching them wrestle and wrangle my mother down the stairs as she literally walked on the ceiling, and as they were used as pawns—either ignorantly or apathetically—against me as a teenager by my mom. Think about how those experiences defined what police represent to me in terms of emotion and experience, how those memories of police became tinted through my particular lenses.

Now, look at those same experiences objectively. The police were involved in a high-speed chase with someone wanted for a crime. While that person was fleeing, they committed even more crimes and killed themselves and my Uncle. What were the cops supposed to do, just let him get away? I suspect my Granny would have felt very different about the situation if the suspect had murdered Billie and the cops had decided to let him get away because it was dangerous. The night the cops took my mother out of the house, she was obviously having a personal crisis, either emotional, drugs, alcohol, or all three. If the police hadn't intervened, she likely would have hurt me, my grandparents, herself, or all of us. Even when assisting with the kidnapping, the officers followed the court's direction. While I believe they legally might have had some discretion regarding how to go about their service, they never could have just ignored the orders.

Knowing my early history with the police and adding my objective insight into what happened during the past events, how would you imagine an interaction with officers would go for me today? This is an example of how the perceptions and emotions surrounding past events have real consequences today. Despite understanding that none of my slanted perspectives towards police are reasonable, I still have them. It still affects me; if I get pulled over, I have to take an extra breath to remain calm. I have to do this despite knowing I almost certainly have earned the traffic stop. This continued anger and my adaptation to it are testaments that our memories will always exist inside us. It doesn't matter whether they are accurate or not or even if they are rational at all—sometimes the best strategy is to be aware of how false those memories might be and adapt.

These two different versions of my memories and how I have dealt with them are examples of "Replacement Logic." Replacement logic is ultimately another way of thinking and is a result of our past experiences. Typically, the experiences that build our unique replacement logic are traumatic, but not always. However, they always owe their origins to incredibly impactful events, regardless of the exact circumstances. They are easily identified as ways of thinking, or more correctly, conclusions of thought contrary to traditionally held views. These conclusions are things the holder knows and accepts as absolute fact despite rational and reasonable evidence to the contrary. We often disguise the nature of this replacement logic by calling them lessons. This somehow has the illusion of letting us off the hook as to their truthfulness or accuracy instead of allowing us to focus on the results.

The previous example of my feeling towards police isn't rational, nor is it supported by the fact in any way, but for me, it exists as its own truth. These replacement logics are powerful. Even when I approach a situation fully aware one exists, and it is likely to impact a given circumstance, I can still find myself unable to steer away or avoid the inevitable. Much like Marty McFly couldn't back down once being called a "Chicken," I can't help but prove wrong anyone who doubts my abilities.

No amount of therapy or contrary experience can overcome these replacement logics; once manifested in our behaviors, they seem to be there forever. While we can never seem to get rid of them, we do have a few tools at our disposal to manage them. A popular but temporary option is to bury them deep down in the dark recesses of our minds. The catch with burying them is no matter how much junk you place on top to hide them, they are always just below, waiting to come out. Their tendency to come out often manifests at rather inopportune times and circumstances. We all have heard about the person who has just "lost it" and went "crazy," seemingly with no warning or other indicators that they were capable of such behavior.

The other option is a little scary but very effective: you embrace the Replacement Logic; accept it exists, and openly manage it with frequent practice and self-awareness. Eventually, you learn to harness it into something infinitely more valuable. Some of these transformations in thinking are easy; for example, what I did with cleaning my mom's trailer and my career. It is straightforward to see how something that, by every measure, was terrible and harmful to my psyche was pretty easy to turn into something positive. Some experiences resist being redefined more than others. I am still trying to rationalize precisely what positive replacement logic I can take away from the raccoon scandal of 1997.

How is it that a terrible thing like cleaning up after my mom's death helps me, but an objective understanding of past police interactions cripples me in another? I don't have the answer to that—if I did, you would be reading this same book but from five times bestselling author Justin White and not just plain Justin White.

The only thing I can offer in the way of answers is that there are none. There is no hard and fast test on whether the water fountain is objectively cold or if you only remember it that way. I can only advise you to stop trying to fight who you are and instead embrace yourself and everything that makes you "you" as you turn your obstacles into steppingstones.

PROOF IT HAPPENED

Visit

A Replacement Son.com

For a full interactive timeline including pictures and documents used in researching and verifying the events in the book.

You can also find links to video of the Amish Sawmill in full operation.

There are contact forms and links to Mr. Whites other business and partnered organizations.

There is also information on how you can have Mr. White speak at your next event.

Made in the USA
Columbia, SC
05 May 2022